Getting
to the
HEART
of the
Matter

Getting
to the
HEART
of the
Matter

*How to Resolve Ongoing Conflicts
in Your Marriage Once and for All*

Dr. Paul Coleman

BOB ADAMS, INC.
Holbrook, Massachusetts

Published by Bob Adams, Inc., 260 Center Street, Holbrook, MA 02343

ISBN: 1-55850-387-0

Printed in the United States of America.

J I H G F E D C B A

Library of Congress Cataloging-in-Publication Data
Coleman, Paul W.
　　Getting to the heart of the matter : how to resolve ongoing conflicts in your marriage once and for all /
Paul Coleman.
　　　　p.　　cm.
　　Includes bibliographical references and index.
　　ISBN 1-55850-387-0
　　1. Marriage. 2. Interpersonal conflict. I. Title.
　　HQ734.C5967 1994
　　646.7'8—dc20　　　　　　　　　　　　　　　　　　　　　　94-15480
　　　　　　　　　　　　　　　　　　　　　　　　　　　　　　　　CIP

This publication is designed to provide accurate and authoritative information with regard to the subject matter covered. It is sold with the understanding that the publisher is not engaged in rendering legal, accounting, or other professional advice. If legal advice or other expert assistance is required, the services of a competent professional person should be sought.
　— From a *Declaration of Principles* jointly adopted by a Committee of the American Bar Association and a Committee of Publishers and Associations

Cover design: Marshall Henrichs

This book is available at quantity discounts for bulk purchases.
For information, call 1-800-872-5627.

For my wife, Jody,
And our children—
Luke, Anna, and Julia

You are in my heart, and you will always matter.

Table of Contents

Part One

Part Two

Part One

Chapter 1

Secrets of the Successful Couple

Believe this: The odds of your marriage becoming *more satisfying and more fulfilling, and requiring less work to succeed,* are higher than magazine articles and television talk shows would have you believe. For example, according to conventional wisdom, marital infidelity is commonplace. Newspaper reports often cite statistics showing that between 30 and 60 percent of marriages will eventually produce an unfaithful partner. New evidence indicates that *those statistics are untrue.* In 1989 the Gallup organization, in conjunction with *Psychology Today* magazine, conducted the first and only scientifically valid survey to measure marital fidelity. The study was a landmark but virtually ignored by the media. Their findings? *Ninety percent* of all married partners remain faithful. While the divorce rate has held steady at 50 percent for the past ten years (even higher for couples previously divorced), as you read this, *two out of every three currently married couples are still married to their first mates.* And according to the Gallup Survey, when asked, "If you could do it all over again would you marry the same person?" 88 percent of all respondents answered, "*Yes.*"

Despite its faults, the institution of marriage is desired by over 90 percent of Americans, most of whom eventually do marry. And those marriages that survive without divorce seem to age well. Partners view one another as best friends. Erotic passion diminishes a bit, but sexual expression becomes more tender, playful, and sometimes more inventive.

Is marriage hard work? Well, it does require sacrifice and is not hassle-free. But many people mistakenly believe that the principle that applies to members of Alcoholics Anonymous—that ill-health is just around the corner and that one must work hard day by day to remain healthy—also applies to married couples. The truth is that thriving marriages are like a bountiful garden. They require attention and nourishment, and on occasion a weed must be pulled. But even if the garden is neglected awhile, it doesn't require exhaustive, frustrating effort to have it looking great again. Healthy gardens, like healthy marriages, are robust and resilient. The secret is *determination.* Successful couples are determined to make their marriage prosper and keep it prospering. And determined couples instinctively cultivate the attitudes and qualities bound to make their goal a reality. Simply put, they love one another as if they mean it. What are their secrets?

The Right Stuff: Four Habits of Determined Couples

Money was tight for Ted and Jenny. To complicate matters, Ted wasn't happy with Jenny's spending habits. She thought she was being cost-conscious, waiting for sales and buying regularly needed products in bulk. He thought she made it difficult for them to meet their monthly expenses.

"The problem," said Ted, "is that she thinks waiting for a sale justifies the expenditure. But I say 'Why must you buy it at all?' Unless it's absolutely essential, I think she should spend less."

"Ted is right," said Jenny. "I do sometimes spend money—even on a good deal—that I could pass up. But Ted isn't aware of the many times I don't buy things. He only sees what I bring home, not what I would have liked to bring home."

At first Jenny coped with Ted's complaints by vowing to spend money on nothing but essentials, a promise that was impractical and soon broken. When she spent money that Ted might think was wasteful, she became secretive, not always telling him of her expenditures. Ted, who tended to scrutinize her shopping lists and credit card charges, usually discovered her hidden bills and became even more scrutinizing, which prompted Jenny to be even more secretive. In sum, Jenny's "solution" to the problem was to watch expenses carefully but also to hide the truth from Ted when necessary. And it made the problem worse. Ted's "solution" was to watch Jenny carefully and become more suspicious when he thought she was being evasive about her spending habits. That too made the problem worse.

Successful couples, determined to make their marriage work, sometimes find themselves in the vicious cycle Ted and Jenny found themselves in. In a vicious cycle, one partner applies a "solution" to a marital problem. If the solution fails, it is not abandoned but *reapplied more intensively,* usually aggravating the very condition it was intended to soothe. It is akin to the philosophy, "If the Coke machine doesn't work, kick it. If it still doesn't work, kick it harder." Over time, you end up with a battered machine.

Successful couples realize that when a solution isn't working, it's time to reassess the problem.

Habit One

Successful couples don't re-apply failed solutions. Instead, they discuss the issue in greater depth and come up with a solution that is mutually agreed upon and meets at least some of each one's needs. (It's a common finding that virtually all failed solutions, and certainly those solutions that only worsen the problem, were applied unilaterally—out of frustration—without much discussion or agreement.)

Frustrated couples apply and reapply solutions that are "more of the same." This is particularly true when a marital problem has become chronic. Couples who cry, "Here we go again," and who fight the same ol' fight continue to act in ways that have been shown in the past to be unhelpful and usually counterproductive. But still they do it.

Ted and Jenny were a determined couple, so they reassessed their problem.

"I guess what bothers me is that I don't feel good about my wages," said Ted. "I wish I could earn more and I do worry about making ends meet, but I don't know what other kind of work I could do. I know I complicate matters by scrutinizing everything Jenny does with money. I think I'd rest easier if we had a minimum amount in our savings that we never fell below. If I knew we always had $2,000 tucked away, I'd be less worried about how much she spends."

So Ted introduced two new factors in their ongoing problem. First, having little money at the end of the month made him feel inadequate as a wage earner. Second, he worried about not having saved enough for "a rainy day."

Jenny continued. "I think what bothers me is Ted not trusting my judgment. The truth is, many times he complained about my spending but later was grateful. For instance, last year I had all the Christmas shopping done by September. Bargain buying resulted in us saving about $300. I'd like him to give me the benefit of the doubt. I promise that on items over fifty dollars I'll talk with him first, but it would mean a lot to me if he didn't ask about the smaller stuff. And yes, I can agree to always keeping $2,000 in our savings account."

With a bit more discussion, they agreed to the following plan: Ted would stop the nit-picking and Jenny would keep her spending above board (no hidden credit card bills). They agreed to keep a minimum of $2,000 in their savings. Ted also agreed to praise Jenny more often, since most of the time her spending habits were helpful. And Jenny noted that she doesn't show her appreciation for how hard Ted works for their money, and promised to correct that.

A hidden benefit to the problem-solving approach of successful couples is that they are not further encumbered by the bad feelings that always develop when a frustrated partner "kicks harder." Frustrated couples always have at least two problems: **the original problem or disagreement, and the resentment and hurt feelings that develop when improper "solutions" are repeatedly and punishingly applied, and the original problem lingers.**

By recognizing early that a "solution" isn't working, and by caring more about working the problem out than about stubbornly getting their way, successful couples don't develop bad feelings. And if they do, those feelings don't remain.

Habit Two

Successful couples give their partner the benefit of the doubt and are more likely to attribute a spouse's annoying behavior to extenuating circumstances than to a character flaw.

Let's say your mate is in a foul mood. Or perhaps he seems standoffish these days, more interested in watching television than in spending time with you or the kids. Or maybe he just said something hurtful and insensitive. Would you probably think something like this:

> *Gee, I wonder what's bothering him?*
> *Maybe his headache is bothering him again.*
> *He's probably tired.*

Or, would you think something like this:

> *Can't he think of anybody but himself?*
> *There he goes again. Sometimes I wonder how I could have married a person like him.*
> *Just because he's had a lousy day at work is no excuse to be miserable to the rest of us. When will he grow up?*

Happy and successful couples will get annoyed with their mates from time to time, but they are more upset with the behavior than with the person. And they are likely to attribute those negative behaviors to external conditions.

In contrast, *frustrated couples don't give their partner the benefit of the doubt; instead they doubt the benefits of their partner.*

Now consider the opposite scenarios. Imagine your mate is particularly attentive or considerate. Or maybe he holds your hand while walking the mall—something he hasn't done in years. Or perhaps you accuse him of something, and instead of becoming angry and defensive, he says, "You're right, Honey. I'm sorry." Would you think

> *I'm lucky to have a man like him.*

Or instead would you think

> *It's about time he showed me some consideration. Then again, he's probably being nice just so I won't insist he attend the barbecue at my parent's house next weekend.*

When considering a partner's positive actions, successful couples will attribute those behaviors to character traits ("*He's a thoughtful person*"). They will view negative behaviors as due to extenuating circumstances ("*He's upset over losing the account at work*").

Frustrated couples do the opposite. They attribute their mate's positive behaviors to extenuating circumstances ("*He's only in a good mood because he won twenty dollars at the office pool*"), and attribute their mate's negative behaviors to character traits ("*He's cold and unfeeling*").

By casting an unfavorable light on their mate, partners in a frustrating relationship rarely see a mate's good intentions and frequently feel worse than the situation calls for. See "Marriage Matters" below to find out.

♥ ♥ ♥

MARRIAGE MATTERS

Researchers Jacqueline Schacter and Dan O'Leary wanted to know whether the *intent* of a spouse's words or actions (e.g., "I think we'll arrive sooner if you turn left here") matched the impact those words or actions had on their partner ("Why must you always criticize my driving?").

Spouses were asked to discuss an area of concern and rate how positive or negative they believed their statements were. They were also asked to rate how positive or negative was the *impact* their mate's words had on them.

The findings? Spouses tend to view the *intent* of their words as slightly more positive (or slightly less negative) than the resulting impact the words actually had. The discrepancy in intent versus impact made little difference to happy couples, since most of their conversations were positive. But unhappy couples responded more negatively to their partner's comments, which only added to their communication difficulties.

The upshot? You may have good intentions, but if your words wound your partner, it's better to apologize than to criticize your mate for being too sensitive. And if you've been hurt by your partner's words or actions, consider the possibility that his intentions were more positive than you gave him credit.

♥ ♥ ♥

Perhaps the more important reason to give your partner the benefit of the doubt has to do with a principle in social psychology research. Essentially, *your view of another person can become self-fulfilling.* If you respond positively to a mate's considerate act, he'll likely do more of the same. If you are critical and hard to satisfy, he'll likely distance himself from you emotionally, which will make you more critical and harder to satisfy.

Pete held a negative (and as is typically the case for frustrated couples, somewhat unfair) view of his wife Pam. He believed that if he raised a marital issue with her, or disagreed with her about something, she'd get angry and defensive. So when Pete was upset with Pam, he thought to himself, *I'd better not say anything. If I do she'll just get mad.* By saying nothing to Pam, Pete concluded that he successfully avoided an argument and thus *reaffirmed his belief that Pam becomes angry and defensive.*

Now think carefully about this. In that scenario, Pam did nothing wrong at all—in fact, she was totally unaware of what was bothering Pete—but nevertheless Pete strengthened his negative conviction about her, and she never had the opportunity to show him he might be mistaken. Of course, Pete will eventually openly disagree with her about something, and chances are he'll be so miffed that he's had to hold back previous concerns that he'll speak to her in a more critical manner. She'll probably detect that he's more critical than he needs to be for the topic at hand and get angry and defensive.

And so it goes.

Habit Three

Successful couples don't allow resentment or misunderstandings to stand in the way of a cooperative effort to make matters right.

If a marital problem keeps recurring, couples understandably become frustrated. But if they're not careful, they will then tell themselves that their partner isn't trying hard enough, further building their resentment. The reality is, both partners are typically working *too hard* on their problems—making sacrifices, holding their tongues, compromising, struggling to avoid conflict—*yet receive no acknowledgment or appreciation for their ongoing efforts.* Lack of appreciation intensifies their resentment and increases the likelihood of emotional flare-ups. Misunderstood, unappreciated, and locked in a stubborn standoff, frustrated couples often regard cooperative behavior by their partners as *"too little, too late."* (That is the polite term used. The attitude most often conveyed, however, is "Screw you.") In other words, *frustrated spouses withdraw in contempt precisely when their partner is willing to cooperate.* Eventually, the "cooperative" partner stops cooperating at approximately the same time the "uncooperative" partner is willing to participate. Is it just bad timing? Are they simply incompatible? out-of-sync? never meant to be together? No. The dynamic that is operating goes something like this:

Step 1 The "uncooperative" partner is angry over past injustices and misunderstandings. Noticing his mate is now trying to work things out, he knows he can afford to be difficult, because she at least is trying to keep the marriage afloat.

Step 2 His stubbornness eventually annoys her (after all, she views herself as having been mistreated and misunderstood too) and she starts to back away, shaking her head in the growing conviction that she's married to a child.

Step 3 He senses she is beginning to get "uncooperative" and decides it is time to be magnanimous and offer some gesture of goodwill. (In truth, he's scared that he let his uncooperative stance go too far.)

Step 4 She senses his fear, and her courage and righteous indignation grow. Like a bird of prey she goes in for the kill. Angry and defiant, she knows she can afford to be difficult, because now *he* is invested in working matters out.

Step 5 The two do battle and eventually retreat to separate corners, taking a break from fighting (but never quite enjoying each other's company, either) until one of them gets scared that the marriage is withering and offers an olive branch, and the other decides it's time to be stubborn. The cycle begins anew at Step One.

As you might imagine, the more often this pattern of non-cooperation repeats itself, the more hurt and pessimistic the couple becomes. Successful couples won't allow the cycle to repeat. Mutual cooperation is the guiding rule, not taking turns at being uncooperative.

Habit Four

Successful couples recognize when they are breaking the rules of proper communication and endeavor to discuss matters respectfully.

While it's true that couples in conflict don't typically use good communication skills, the skills required are not obscure and hard to understand. Many make common sense. Don't interrupt. Try not to complain about more than one or two issues at once. No name calling. No mind reading. Avoid provocative gestures (finger pointing, rolling one's eyes in contempt, walking away in disgust, etc.). Ironically, by making an effort to fight fair and communicate respectfully (in other words, by attempting to show one another they care), successful couples can get away with breaking the rules once in a while. As I showed in my book *The 30 Secrets of Happily Married Couples,* happy couples *interrupt each other more often than unhappy couples.* They also mind-read as often as unhappy couples. But because they get along well and demonstrate mutual caring, interruptions and mind reading are viewed as signs of interest. Unhappy couples view them as rude and intrusive.

Frustrated couples break the rules of communication and fair fighting. Often they do so knowing at the time they are only making matters worse. But they find it difficult to stop.

Breaking the rules isn't limited to displays of anger and disrespect. Listen to this couple:

> She: "Do you like the casserole?"
> He: "I'm eating it, aren't I?"

> She (later on): "Do you really want to see this play?"
> He: "I bought the tickets, didn't I?"

> She (later in bed): "Do you love me?"
> He: "I'm still here, aren't I?"

On the surface, their very brief conversations were somewhat polite, but there was obviously an undercurrent of worry or aggravation that wasn't being addressed. In this case, the wife asked questions that reflected doubts she was having of his interest in her. She was really probing for some sign that their relationship was alive and kicking. But she didn't say what was really on her mind. The husband sensed he was being tested in some way and he didn't like it. He also thought that her questions placed him in a no-win position. If he answered that he did want to attend the play, she would doubt him—which is in fact exactly what she did do. If he answered he did not want to attend the play, she'd get angry—or so he convinced himself. His irritation with her was obvious, but he didn't discuss it. Consequently, she periodically scanned his psyche to ascertain what was *really* going on inside his head, and he continued to use language that on the surface indicated his contentment, but that really masked his anger. Each one was aware of not being totally frank with the other, but they continued their unproductive style of communication.

How Determined Are You?

To make your marriage work, two factors are essential. One is a strong *desire* to have a successful relationship; the second is a strong *willingness* to do what is required to make a successful relationship.

Successful couples have strong and positive answers to the following two questions:

- **On a scale of 1 to 10 (a 10 indicating maximum desire), how much do you want your relationship to succeed?**
- **On a scale of 1 to 10 (a 10 indicating maximum effort) how much effort are you willing to put forth to insure that your relationship succeeds?**

Answer each question with a number from 1 to 10. Then multiply the two answers (maximum possible score is 100). As a general rule, very successful couples score 70 or higher. As the score drops below 50, frustration, stubbornness, and pessimism have infiltrated the relationship and will impede, but not prevent, success. As the score goes below 20, one or both partners have seriously considered ending the relationship, and commitment to the marriage is half-hearted, at best.

At scores of 50 or below, it is crucial that two things happen soon. First, the negative and hurtful interactions must halt. Calling a "time-out" from conflict is better than continuing to hurt one another. It has been shown in research that "pushing each other's buttons" or negative interactions of any kind far outweigh the benefit of kind and considerate actions. One prominent researcher estimated that the impact of five to ten positive interactions is canceled out by one negative interaction, when the relationship is already unsatisfying. Putting some arguments on the back burner may be necessary for a while. And if a discussion starts to turn sour, it is wise to say something like, "I don't intend to argue. I want us to be able to talk, not fight. Bear with me, I'm not good at this yet."

A second important requirement, when your Determination Score falls below 50, is to increase positive, caring gestures. (See "Building a Successful Relationship," below.) Author Stephen Covey recommends making deposits into what he calls your Emotional Bank Account. Acts of kindness, honesty, respect, and thoughtfulness help you build up a positive reserve that can help "pay" for the occasional unkind or disrespectful remark. If the Emotional Bank Account is overdrawn, trust is low and tension is high. You walk on eggshells. Communication becomes a series of strategic maneuvers. A build-up of capital in the Emotional Bank Account, combined with a dramatic reduction in the frequency of hurtful interactions, are two immediate requirements for couples low on the Determination Scale. It isn't easy, because by definition such couples are not fully invested in one another by that point. But it is an essential first step to success.

BUILDING A SUCCESSFUL RELATIONSHIP

It's essential to invest and reinvest in your marriage bonds.

1. You are already doing thoughtful and considerate things for your mate, I'm sure. Identify what you do already and *do those things more often*. Remember, the little things mean a lot. More lunch dates, more kisses, more breakfasts in bed, cleaning the car more often, complimenting her appearance—all can make a difference.

2. Psychologists Ellyn Bader and Peter Pearson recommend asking your spouse, "What is one thing I can do for you today that would make your day go easier or help you feel more special?" Then do it.

Remember, it helps a lot when you

- keep your promises
- act thoughtfully and politely
- tell your spouse what you'd like from him—don't wait for him to guess

♥ ♥ ♥

The Argument Audit:
Identifying The Three Stages of Conflict

While it appears that some arguments come from nowhere, the truth is that couple conflict follows a fairly predictable pattern. Once you understand the pattern, you can more easily make changes to reduce the likelihood of hurt feelings, misunderstandings, and unproductive arguments.

But first, fill in your responses to the *Argument Audit* below. Your total score will help you identify which stage of conflict you are in.

The Argument Audit

Please mark your scores in the space provided at the end of each item. Use the following scale:

Rarely 0
Sometimes 1
Often 2
Much of the time 3

When you complete all the items, tally the individual scores. Compare your final score to the key presented at the bottom.

1. Do you feel you must assess your mate's mood before you feel free to speak to him/her? _____

2. Do the same arguments/conflicts occur repeatedly? _____

3. Do you feel out of sync with each other emotionally? (For example, when he's ready for talking or lovemaking, you're not—and vice versa.) _____

4. Are you accused of overreacting (or underreacting) to his/her behaviors or attitudes? _____

5. When the relationship seems to be going well, do you anticipate problems on the horizon? _____

6. Are you more invested in your spouse's changing some aspect of his/her behavior than he/she is? _____

7. When you believe that some problems in the relationship are improving, do you view a setback as "back to square one"? _____

8. When you and your mate have a disagreement, do you react more to his/her manner (tone of voice, attitude) than to the specifics of the disagreement? _____

9. Do you get defensive or offensive with your mate? _____

10. Do you anticipate (correctly or incorrectly) what your mate will say or do before it happens? _____

11. Do you act on those assumptions before checking them out with your mate? _____

12. Do you feel threatened that your mate has (or might be interested in having) some separate interests or hobbies? _____

13. Does one or both of you avoid discussing areas of conflict, or does at least one of you withdraw from such a discussion prematurely? _____

14. Do you feel responsible for your mate's feelings/actions to the extent that, if he/she is feeling blue, you wonder what you might have done to cause it? _____

15. Do you ever worry about being disowned by your parents, or that they might cut you off from them emotionally? _____

Score

0-10 No problems or Stage One only. Major problems will be avoided or caught early enough to resolve.

11-25 Stage One-Stage Two. Problems are developing but can be nipped in the bud or resolved readily.

26-35 Stage Two. Some problems have become difficult or unmanageable. Solutions do exist.

36-45 Stage Three. Probably many unresolved problems. Marital satisfaction is low. A committed effort to resolve issues is absolutely essential.

The Three Stages of Conflict

Stage One

At this stage, either there are no problems in the relationship that make a difference, or they are at the "precognitive" level—that is, problems are beginning to brew, but awareness of them is minimal. A perceptive spouse might inquire, "Is something the matter?" but be satisfied if she is told, "No, nothing is the matter." Often at Stage One, clues to potential problems are evident. If identified early, the problems can be nipped in the bud. For example, Kim and Todd had recently gotten married. But Todd spent much of his free time with his old friends instead of with Kim. Typically, newlyweds build a cocoon around themselves, detaching somewhat from family and old friends, and bonding with one another. But Todd's behavior was out of the ordinary. He was trying to conduct his life *as if he were still single.* Kim finally spoke with him about her worries and Todd was receptive.

"My friends warned me that once I got married I wouldn't have any say over what I wanted to do," Todd explained. "I guess I wanted to show them that just because I'm married I haven't lost my independence. But maybe you're right. I went too far."

Kim and Todd were a determined couple and were able to resolve the matter. Not all couples are so fortunate.

Stage Two

This is the pivotal stage. If the problems weren't nipped in Stage One, at Stage Two they have now become obvious and a bit troublesome. Here, attempts are made to resolve the problems. *A successful couple will discuss the problem until they understand all of its dimensions, and arrive at a solution that meets one another's needs. Then they will give the solution an honest try and discuss how well it's working.* If it's not working, they'll reassess the problem and arrive at a new solution.

Frustrated couples falter at this stage. First, they may not even discuss the problem. Instead, on her own one partner will determine what she thinks is the nature of the problem and implement a solution she thinks is reasonable (*There he goes again, being stubborn and unreasonable when I tell him my opinion* [identification of the problem]. *So screw him. I'll just sit and be quiet and avoid him the rest of the day* [the solution]. But what if she misidentified the problem? Or what if her spouse doesn't like her solution? Let's say that when Kim noticed her new husband, Todd, was spending more time with his high school buddies than with her, she thought, *He's not attracted to me anymore.* Let's say her "solution" was to join the health club and exercise four nights a week after work—time she'd usually make available for Todd. Let's also say that she decides she must lose ten pounds and thus refuses to go out to dinner—something she and Todd might ordinarily do twice a month. To Todd, Kim has suddenly lost interest in him. He may even begin to wonder, *Is she meeting some other guy at the health club? She never tried to get herself in shape like that for me before . . .*

By not discussing their concerns and taking matters into their own hands, Kim and Todd made one problem into many.

At Stage Two, solutions that don't work are not usually abandoned but intensified. Remember the "kick the Coke machine" example? Misunderstandings and bad feelings take root at this stage, so that even if a problem finally gets resolved, hurt feelings can linger.

Couples can get stuck in Stage Two, like being trapped on a merry-go-round. Frustration over unresolved issues leads to criticism, stubbornness, or withdrawal, which intensifies the frustrations and bad feelings that make problems more difficult to resolve, and so on.

The longer one is at Stage Two, the more likely blaming one's spouse will replace a willingness to make an honest evaluation of one's own role in the problem.

Stage Three

Here, annoyance and resentment have been replaced by bitterness. What little empathy one spouse had for the other is quickly evaporating. Couples still together at this stage either agree to ignore one another as often as possible, or they insist that for the marriage to survive the other partner must change. Marital therapy may be the only option for couples entrenched in Stage Three.

The Making of the Successful Couple

Successful couples are bred, not born. And in most cases, although childhood experiences can have an impact on how one behaves in a marriage, the evolving nature of the couple's relationship has more of an impact on whether a couple will be determined to make their marriage work, or frustrated and ill-motivated.

In other words, if you are not a successful couple you can still become one. The rest of this book will help you to do just that.

Keep in Mind

Successful couples:

- Don't reapply solutions that didn't work. Instead, they reassess the problem and arrive at a new, mutually agreed-upon solution.
- Give partners the benefit of the doubt. They are not quick to criticize but are quick to empathize.
- Are willing to cooperate even if their spouse has been uncooperative.
- Recognize when they are breaking the rules of effective communication and try to correct their mistake.
- Tend to nip problems before they get out of hand.
- Instinctively understand that "winning" an argument or needing to be "right" about an issue is a loss for the relationship and is the wrong thing to do.

Chapter 2

Six Hidden Clues to Upcoming Marital Problems

In chapter 1 you learned that conflicts can evolve into three stages. In the first stage, opportunities exist to halt problems before they take hold. But not every marital problem will be nipped in the bud, and there are two simple reasons for that.

One reason is that some problems truly are bolts from the blue. Events such as a sudden and permanent deterioration of physical health due to illness or injury; job loss and extended unemployment; even an unplanned pregnancy force a couple to contend with circumstances they never anticipated. While adversity can ultimately strengthen a relationship, it often has the immediate effect of straining the fibers that hold the marriage in place.

Carol and Tom were married eleven years when Carol dropped her bombshell: "Tom, I know we decided long ago we wouldn't have children. And I always believed I never wanted to be a mother. But I know now I was wrong. I do want children. And I don't think I can be really happy in this marriage if you can't support me on this."

Tom was blindsided. A future he always anticipated was suddenly shattered. He could have a marriage with Carol or a childless marriage, but he couldn't have both. (Tom and Carol eventually resolved this problem. See chapter 7.)

So some problems do burst on the scene uninvited. But the primary reason why many partners won't nip problems in the bud is not that the early-warning signs aren't there—they are. But the spouses want to *pretend* that problems or concerns don't exist between them. They *ignore* the tell-tale signs of a brewing conflict. Or if they do acknowledge those signs, they *make excuses* to maintain the illusion that the marriage is like a high-priced linoleum floor: tough, shiny, and virtually maintenance-free . . .

Signs of Distress

The more obvious indicators of marital distress:

- You dislike some of your partner's behaviors or attitudes but believe you can change him.

- You rationalize *recurrent*, problematic behavior (e.g. "He doesn't mean to be hurtful. He's just under a lot of pressure").

- You frequently react hotly to a minor issue.
- Your negative feelings (sadness, anger, nervousness) are too intense, while your positive feelings (happiness, enthusiasm, optimism) seem blunted.
- You experience a growing sense of entitlement.
- You have difficulty expressing your viewpoint without being challenged by your spouse.
- You walk on eggshells.
- There is an increase in your fault finding, with a corresponding decrease in your capacity to empathize with your mate.
- Arguments/disagreements often contain the following: bringing up the past; complaining, "You always . . ." or "You never . . ."; name calling (*"irresponsible," "childish," "selfish," "insensitive,"* etc.).
- You resent it when your spouse gets his way.
- You can't quite forgive and forget.

Putting marital concerns on the table is always a bit uncomfortable. But most people want to protect the image that they are lovable, acceptable, and in control of their thoughts, feelings, behaviors, and destiny. Unfortunately, conflict resolution requires talking things out—which means taking the chance that your partner might not love you, might reject you, and might say or do something that makes you feel more helpless and less in control of matters. Consequently, the growing problems between you and your mate (which are more and more obvious to the kids, in-laws, and family pet) are too readily put aside. If you only contend with marital problems when they have grown large and unmanageable, you've waited too long and may no longer possess the patience to deal with them cleanly. By waiting, you allow blaming to replace honest self-appraisal, accusations to replace constructive dialogue, hurt to replace contentment, and biased perceptions ("She just doesn't care!") to replace clarity and level-headedness. But at least now you admit there really is a problem. Ironically, by having pretended no problems existed when problems obviously did, you now run a greater risk of damaging what you always wanted to protect: your happiness, your sense of lovability, your sense of control, your children, and your relationship.

And it didn't have to happen that way.

How to Prevent Some Problems from Ever Happening: Hidden Clues and Hidden Solutions

Mike and Cindy have been happily married for almost two years. But in the past six months, Mike has experienced a vague "closed in" feel-

ing. He handles it by spending a bit more time away from Cindy. He thinks she hasn't noticed.

Olivia and Sean have two kids, a newly refinanced low-interest mortgage, and a satisfying relationship. But Olivia finds herself in the middle of other people's troubled marriages—fretting, disapproving, and offering advice. Does that provide a clue to her feelings about her own marriage?

"But I cleaned up after the puppy last time!" complained Carl to his wife. Well, fair is fair, but his complaint is also a tell-tale sign of a bigger problem . . .

In these three examples, each spouse would probably proclaim that his or her marriage is satisfying . . . for the most part. Yet, like cracks in the foundation, their minor concerns are really precursors to predictable—and troublesome—marital difficulties. The warning signs are there. Will they recognize them? And will they know what to do to prevent future problems?

In the first example, Mike withdrew from Carol to ease his sense of being smothered. Research evidence is clear that a husband's withdrawal from conversation is a prelude to marital dissatisfaction over the following few years. And persons who routinely try to avoid conflict (via withdrawal or silence) sow the seeds for future conflict and unhappiness. (There is a better way for Mike to get the space he craves. See "Hidden Clue Two.")

Olivia's concerns about other people's marriages and Carl's complaint that it's his wife's turn to clean up after the puppy each signify that their currently satisfying marriages may be headed for some rocky times. (See "Hidden Clue Three" and "Hidden Clue Four.")

As these examples suggest, *the absence of conflict is not always a clear indication that the marriage is on the right track.* It is safe to say that virtually everyone who gets married does so with the belief that they will make their marriage work. Newlyweds are usually gloriously happy and in love, but still almost 20 percent of those couples who eventually break up will do so within the first two years of marriage. Those spouses may have thought they could read their partner like a book, but they obviously missed the fine print.

Most people enter into a marriage with no formal training in what marriage is really about. (Hair stylists have more training than most newlyweds.) Society expects us to learn how to relate by osmosis: Watching our parents interact and learning how to get along with siblings and school mates is somehow supposed to provide us with all we need to know. But many parents were not good husband-wife role models, even if they were loving and committed parents. And our school mates were just kids themselves. What did they know?

Thus, many couples learn how to negotiate and resolve conflicts by trial and error. Those who succeed develop the confidence that their marriage is sound and their conflict-resolution skills finely honed. But too many couples don't succeed in resolving their conflicts. Many others—perhaps the majority—have acceptable but mixed results, and a marriage that could stand a bit more happiness.

♥ ♥ ♥
MARRIAGE MATTERS

A 1989 Gallup Survey revealed that, while about 60 percent of the respondents rated their marriage as "very happy," only about 65 percent of the "very happy" people said their spouse made them feel important or respected their opinion. About one-third of all respondents rated their marriage as just "pretty happy" and another one-third indicated that at least once they were prepared to leave their mate.

You're not alone. Seems like many couples struggle a bit with making their marriage work.

♥ ♥ ♥

The good news is that many relationship problems can be headed off at the pass. And successful couples often do just that. You needn't have a troubled relationship to know that problems may be on the horizon. When the relationship is still working well, when good feelings abound and hopes are high, there are subtle signs that will tell you whether your marriage is on track or veering slightly off course.

Hidden Clue One

Are you or is your mate disconnected from your family of origin? Or is at least one of you overly connected to your family?

Roger rarely spoke with his father. Roger's parents divorced when he was three, and Roger lived with his father, who eventually remarried. Roger's stepmother was harsh and punitive, but Roger couldn't count on his father to intervene and come to his aid. In Roger's view, his dad was "a wimp who did his best to appease his new wife at all costs, even if it meant allowing me to suffer. I want as little to do with my father as possible."

Now married for the first time, Roger is fiercely loyal to Lily. A successful attorney, Roger was able to shower Lily with gifts when they were dating. Often he went overboard. When she began taking piano lessons, he surprised her by replacing her aged upright with a baby grand Steinway. Restaurants were always the finest. Travel was always first class. And she truly loved him. But problems were on the horizon. Because Roger never felt loved as a child, Lily's love for him filled a cavernous void. With no family to speak of, Lily was his life. And as he reminded her so often when he lavished her with gifts, he expected nothing in return. Of course, that wasn't true. He expected her to be fiercely loyal to him. He expected her to love him unconditionally. And because he secretly feared he was an unlovable person, he expected she might reject him if he ever stopped making so much money. So he continued to work overtime and build his practice, and eventually—as is the case in any marriage—their madly-in-love passion for one another softened. But Roger couldn't tolerate that. Instead of allowing tenderness and caring to fill some of the spaces left by a tired passion, he felt threatened. He became quick to feel unappreciated by Lily. He even wondered whether perhaps she'd been taking advantage of his generosity all this time. His accusations deeply offended her. Roger would apologize, but he couldn't shake the thought that Lily was caring less and less for him and that she was more preoccupied with interests outside the marriage.

When anybody is emotionally cut off from his family of origin, he runs the risk of expecting his spouse to fill the void the family should have filled. Consequently, he can become possessive and easily hurt, quick to see evidence of disloyalty or betrayal when all his partner wished was to have a dollop of independence and to grow as a person.

Conversely, you can be too attached to your family of origin. *If visits or phone calls to parents or siblings are frequent and rigidly adhered to, and if marital quarrels have erupted over this, you are probably too attached.* Family love and loyalty is a wonderful thing. And in a crisis, you may understandably need to spend more time than usual with your parents or siblings. But your marriage needs to be nourished. If the marriage relationship takes second place to one's relationship with one's parents, the marriage can atrophy. Often, a vicious cycle develops when one spouse is too attached to her family, causing marital satisfaction to decline, prompting her to spend even more time with her family, as they increasingly become the main source of comfort and understanding in her life.

Solution: If you are cut off from your family of origin, understand that your expectations of your mate are probably too high and that you are bound to feel severely disappointed by your partner eventually. Any success at reconnecting in a civil manner with your family can help. Healing some of the old wounds is even better but can take time. Your basic tasks in the marriage are twofold: to learn to ease up on the reins of control over your mate (you can truly trust her only if she is free from your coercions or manipulations), and to develop the conviction that you are lovable despite your faults.

If you are too involved with your family of origin, you need to cut back the frequency of your involvement and use the extra time to develop outside interests you find challenging and rewarding. You also need to spend more quality time with your mate.

Hidden Clue Two

Are you or is your mate a conflict avoider?

Your relationship won't be satisfying if one of you picks fights over every little thing, quickly turning sweet dispositions sour. But if you or your mate routinely keeps quiet about concerns so as to avoid an argument, short-term relief will be followed by long-term dissatisfaction. According to researchers Patricia Noller and Mary Anne Fitzpatrick, not only do distressed couples fight more than nondistressed couples, they also *avoid conflict* much more than happier couples. Avoiding conflict is an understandable approach if you have no faith in your conflict-resolution skills. *But most problems must be faced before they can be erased.*

Since even happy couples will avoid hot topics from time to time, how can you tell whether you or your partner is a true-blue conflict avoider? Esteemed researcher John Gottman at the University of Washington suggests you follow these guidelines. Conflict avoiders:

- Don't often turn to their mates for comfort or support when they are feeling blue.
- Are less apt to discuss routine matters such as how their day went. Brief, one-word answers may be all they offer.
- Don't view their mate as their friend.
- Tend to blame their partner and have a difficult time determining the role they play in a marital problem.
- Often hold traditional views of sex roles.
- More often are men.

Remember Mike and Cindy? Mike started feeling a bit smothered, so he quietly carved out more space for himself, distancing himself from Cindy. He didn't tell her what was happening because he didn't want to hurt her feelings. But she noticed his growing detachment, was worried about it, and met resistance when she tried to broach the topic. How could Mike have better handled his sense of being smothered? A simple three-step explanation would have sufficed.

Step One: Express Empathy or Understanding for Your Mate's Position
"Cindy, I guess I didn't mention this because I didn't want to hurt your feelings. I know you like to spend as much time with me as possible . . ."

Step Two: Express Your Need
". . . But sometimes I just need time to myself."

Step Three: Ask for Feedback
"Can we work something out?"

Expressing a need that might compete with your partner's need can be painless as long as each of you shows that you care about your mate's needs, too. Chances are, if Cindy responded to Mike by saying, *"I can understand you want time to yourself. But I would like to watch a movie together tonight,"* Mike would cooperate because he felt understood and accepted.

Conflict avoidance is unwise. But you can learn to overcome it.

Solution: If you and your mate routinely end up arguing as you try to discuss your differences—which therefore causes you to avoid conversation and conflict—your most important problem is your inability to communicate effectively and respectfully. Before you tackle any other problem in the relationship, devote time to improving your communication skills (see chapter 9). If you and your mate get along but you are simply uncomfortable with the prospect of raising difficult topics, you may be doing more harm than good to the relationship. Prefacing discussions with "Bear with me, Sweetheart. I'm just not comfortable talking about some things" helps a lot.

Hidden Clue Three

Are you or is your mate overly involved and worried about someone else's marriage?

Certainly if a friend or relative has a marriage in trouble, you may care and want to offer support wherever possible. But if, like Olivia, you cross a line and become over-involved—if you routinely offer advice, if you feel caught in the middle, if your anger or frustration at one of the other participants interferes with your overall contentment (or your pocketbook—do you loan them money to ease their burdens?)—it may not be *their* marriage that needs your attention.

Contented spouses don't get hooked into someone else's marital woes. For that matter, neither do they get hooked into *any* other problem a friend or relative might have, marital or otherwise. It isn't that happy couples don't care about others. They do care. But they allow others to make their own decisions and to accept responsibility for resolving their predicament. Do you take it personally when the well-intended advice or support you offer is exploited or unappreciated? If so, you're "hooked."

Over-involvement in any activity diminishes your involvement in other areas—your own family, your health, or your peace of mind. And over-involvement may really be a diversion from areas in your personal life that need attention.

Solution: First, be honest. Might the problems you are over-involving yourself in symbolize concerns in your own marriage? If so, it would be better to spend time fixing your own relationship. If friends or relatives try to reinvolve you in their problems, gently refuse either to offer advice or to be a spokesperson for one of them. Keep your comments limited to general phrases like, "I know it isn't easy for you" or "I hope matters improve." Stop offering advice and don't take sides.

Hidden Clue Four

Do you or does your mate show kindness and consideration on an "I'll scratch your back if you scratch mine" basis?

In a 1988 study reported in *The Journal of Marriage and the Family*, spouses who were kind to one another were evaluated over the course of several years. Couples whose kindness was motivated by an "I'll be nice as long as you are nice" attitude broke up within five years.

Remember Carl and his puppy? Carl cleaned up after the puppy the last time and now he complained it was his wife's turn. Sharing household chores is common in a healthy relationship, but keeping close track of who did what for whom is a sign of problems on the horizon. A satisfying marriage requires *flexibility*. Partners must be willing to do more than their fair share some of the time if the relationship is to have room to breathe. In a study of over three hundred married couples, the happiest among them agreed that *you have to be willing to put more into your marriage than you take out.* Very satisfied spouses do believe that, *over time,* the give-and-take of a marriage will be approximately fifty-fifty. But they do not keep track on a chore-by-chore basis.

Couples with a "tit-for-tat" mentality eventually degenerate into "an eye for an eye" mentality. They use retaliation to balance perceived inequities in the relationship. Consequently, each partner becomes the other's competitor, concerned more about "winning" and "being right" than working out their problems to their *mutual* satisfaction. Unable to work together for a common cause, each keeps a ledger book of "wins" and "losses," never understanding that if one spouse must lose for the other to win, then the relationship always loses.

If the "tit-for-tat" mentality developed within the first two years of your relationship, it likely has its roots in your childhood or in a previous relationship. Perhaps you grew up in a home where your needs didn't get met, and now you feel owed. If so, you may be blaming your spouse for not meeting the needs that your parents didn't meet. If your blaming has persisted, you have probably offended your mate, who is now less apt to show caring because he or she feels you have been unfair and unkind.

Solution: Discuss with your partner how your childhood needs didn't get met and apologize for blaming him or her. Once you have done this, each of you is advised to pinpoint about ten things you already do for your mate that you know are helpful and pleasing, and do them more frequently for the next few months. If wounds from former relationships persist, consider talking with a qualified therapist.

Hidden Clue Five

Do you compromise too much in order to keep your mate happy?

For several Fridays in a row, Sarah's office mates went for a drink after work. She wanted to join them but felt guilty that Jim would have to care for their three young children by himself. After all, he was tired after a full work week too. So she came home on time every Friday, never bothering to tell Jim the sacrifice she made for him. When Jim called her one Friday afternoon and announced he would be two hours late because he had decided to hit some golf balls with his buddy, Sarah seethed. *"How could he be so selfish?"* she wondered. *"He didn't seem to care the least little bit that I might be tired and might want him to come home right after work."*

Was Sarah right to be angry? Well, if Jim truly didn't care that his golf playing would inconvenience her, then Sarah had a right to be angry.

But the real problem was that Sarah compromised *too much.* How can you tell? Her hidden sacrifices for Jim came with an unstated price: She expected him to behave similarly. The problem was that Jim was unaware of the "deal" they'd struck. That also made it difficult for him to show appreciation for her sacrifices.

It was considerate of Sarah to think of Jim's needs, and a strong marriage will contain many unseen sacrifices made by willing spouses. But partners need periodic shows of appreciation from one another. If too many of your sacrifices or compromises are *hidden*, you'll eventually resent not getting the appreciation you think you deserve.

Let's say that Jim also has many hidden compromises. Maybe he never spoke up that he'd rather stay home when the family went out for pizza. Maybe he spent some precious leisure time cleaning all the dust from under the beds, so his wife wouldn't throw her back out bending over. And now his buddy invites him to hit some golf balls, and he thinks, *Why not? I deserve it.*

Now imagine that when he returns from golf Sarah is standoffish. He asks what's wrong. She says "Nothing." He doesn't believe her and he says so. Then she tells him he was selfish to go play golf. Will he feel guilty? *No way!* He'll think about all the sacrifices he's made for her and feel he was *entitled* to play golf. Will Sarah feel guilty for accusing him of being selfish? *No way!* She'll think about all the sacrifices she's made for him and feel *entitled* to her anger. And both will be peeved that their mate is being so insensitive to their needs.

If you compromise too often you'll compromise the relationship.

Solution: Speak up periodically about some of your sacrifices to get some credit you deserve. If you resent compromising, you've begun to believe there is an inequity in the relationship. Best to clarify the inequities with your mate before you make too many more hidden sacrifices.

Had Sarah told Jim that she'd like to go out with her office mates after work on an upcoming Friday, she probably would have gone eventually. If Jim complained, then they'd have an opportunity to discuss how each needed to help the other out at home *and* have some time off for good behavior.

Hidden Clue Six

Are you and your mate "opposites?"

Mark is a tad shy, disinclined to introduce himself to others at parties but always gracious and polite when he does speak. Joan is outgoing, flirtatious at times, and not afraid to express an opposing opinion aggressively. Will they make a good couple?

Generally, the more dissimilar you are from your mate, the less you'll have a relationship that works. But too much similarity can be boring and create future dissatisfaction, too. Perhaps the most important similarities that will help you get along have to do with your background. Do you both share the same culture? A similar IQ? Similar religious beliefs and moral values? If so, you increase the odds you'll get along.

Could Mark and Joan hit it off? The more extreme their differences, the less likely their marriage would be to succeed. But let's presume that Joan isn't so flirtatious and that Mark, although slow to warm up, can fit in with a crowd. In that case, despite obvious personality differences, they might make a terrific couple. After all, some differences can help enliven a relationship.

But the real key to making a marriage of opposites work is this: Personality differences don't make a difference when spouses *value their partner's traits* and wish to develop them in their own personalities. For instance, Mark might tell Joan, *"I really admire your ability to be so at ease with people. One day I'd like to work a crowd the way you do."* And Joan might say to Mark, *"I like the fact that you don't always need to be the center of attention to feel content. One day I'd like to feel self-assured the way you do."* Such comments reflect feeling of excitement derived from the other person's differences. In troubled relationships, personality differences are criticized and viewed as roadblocks to fulfillment instead of as pathways to a more multifaceted self.

Solution: If you and your mate have some opposing qualities, that's normal. Your best bet is to determine the benefits of your mate's traits rather than criticize them. Take the most troublesome personality difference, the "logical" spouse and the "emotional" spouse. If you are overly logical, your mate will be frustrated and overly emotional, which will cause you to be even more logical, and so on. A concerted effort to balance logic and emotion will be appreciated.

Keep in Mind

In a healthy relationship . . .

- . . . partners have a positive connection with their families of origin and invest some extra time with them periodically, but always make sure the marital relationship is getting the nourishment it needs to thrive.

- . . . partners will, from time to time, ignore some relationship concerns rather than complain. But if the concerns keep surfacing, successful partners will address them before resentment or hurt feelings begin to fester.

- . . . partners may care "about" someone else's relationship problems (and offer a hand on the shoulder and emotional support) but rarely care "for" the others (by repeatedly offering advice, getting in the middle, and making sacrifices to "help" the hurting party).

- ... partners understand that marriage requires give and take, but that a successful marriage is not always a fifty-fifty proposition. When inequities linger, a mature spouse will not whine, bicker, punish, pout, humiliate, give the "cold-shoulder," or retaliate as a way to even the score. Instead he will speak up about his concerns in an honest, respectful manner.

- ... partners express appreciation for their mate's sacrifices. They rarely feel they've settled for less when they must compromise, because thriving couples realize that if it's good for the relationship, it is good for the individual.

- ... partners are not threatened by their mate's opposite traits but value them to some degree. Becoming a whole person often means trying on various personality traits for size. Healthy couples encourage personal growth and being the best one can be. In such relationships the spouses often outgrow character weaknesses.

Couples with distinct personality differences who value personal growth and development, and who respect their partner's traits, can make their marriage work.

♥ ♥ ♥

MARRIAGE MATTERS

The divorce rate is lower for parents who only have boys than for parents who only have girls. Why? Evidence suggests that fathers spend more time with child care and are more involved in their children's lives overall if they have sons than if they only have daughters. In one study by Maryse Richards and Elena Duckett of Loyola University, 483 mostly white, fifth through ninth graders carried beepers for one week. They were randomly "beeped" seven times a day, at which time they had to report what they were doing, what they were thinking, and what they were feeling. The researchers used that format as a way to measure how often parents were involved in their children's experiences. The results? The more involved a father was with his job, the less involvement he had with his daughters compared to his sons. In fact, the *more satisfaction* a father had with his job, *the lower his daughter's self-esteem* (presumably due in part to his diminished involvement in her life).

Fathers are particularly unlikely to attend to mundane but necessary child care responsibilities, such as taking time off from work to take the child to a pediatrician. A key to marital satisfaction and healthy self-esteem in daughters is to raise the level of paternal involvement in the lives of a father's his children.

♥ ♥ ♥

Chapter 3

The Conflict Styles of Dissatisfied Couples

Steve and Rita had been having marital problems for about six months. Steve, like many men, was not comfortable discussing their difficulties but knew that such conversations were necessary and inevitable. One night he tried to broach the topic of their relationship with Rita.

"I wish we could get along better," he blurted out during dinner. Steve was nervous but felt good about taking the initiative rather than avoiding the topic.

"Me too," Rita said, surprised by Steve's sudden interest in conversation. "But you certainly didn't act like you wanted to get along yesterday when we were driving to your brother's." One of her pet peeves with Steve lately was his on-again/off-again mood to work things out.

"You would have to bring up yesterday, wouldn't you," Steve stormed as he stood up and left the dinner table. To Steve, Rita was being unnecessarily critical, and he responded to her criticism the way he usually did. He withdrew. *It's her fault we can't improve things,* he thought to himself on the way out.

Rita watched him leave, her anger about to bubble over. "How can we solve our problems if you won't let me say what's bothering me," she yelled to him. *It's his fault we can't improve things,* she thought to herself.

Three Counterproductive Attitudes

Steve and Rita's interaction just now was brief, but it illuminated three attitudes they each hold dear—attitudes that couples trapped on the merry-go-round of repetitive conflict often embrace.

1. *"I know the truth."* Rita believed that her view of Steve was accurate. He was uncooperative, inconsistent, and downright wrong in his assessment of their problems.

    Steve admittedly gave lip-service to the idea that Rita had some reasonable views about the problems in their marriage but his actions indicated otherwise. She was wrong and he was right. He saw the truth. She was blind to it.

    According to family therapist W. Robert Beavers, successful couples don't harbor a right-versus-wrong mentality. Such couples understand that "truth" is often relative.

Helpful Guideline: Even if you firmly believe you know the "truth" about a marital situation, it is helpful to focus on the things your spouse says that make some sense *instead of criticizing what you disagree with.*

2. *"My motives are helpful and make perfect sense. Your motives are malicious and unreasonable."*

Steve interpreted Rita's dinnertime comment (about his uncooperative behavior while driving to his brother's house) as motivated by ill-will. He viewed her comment as totally inappropriate, especially since he had tried to discuss their relationship openly and calmly, without hostility. But Rita felt her comment was justified and motivated by a desire to "put the cards on the table" and not just ignore his irksome behaviors. She thought she was being mature and straightforward, not beating around the bush. "My intent wasn't to criticize but to inform," she said. But Steve didn't believe her.

And why did Steve leave the dining room when their discussion had barely begun? "Because I knew if I stayed we'd just get into an argument," he said. "Isn't it better to avoid an argument?" Steve believed his motive was not malicious but that it reflected a concern for the relationship. He didn't want the marriage to deteriorate over yet another argument. But Rita believed he withdrew from the discussion "in order to punish me. In fact, I don't think he really ever intended to have a full and honest talk about our concerns. He just wanted to look like the good guy and make me out to be the bad guy."

Successful couples recognize that their partners may act in hurtful ways but for helpful (albeit misguided) reasons. They look for the noble intent rather than the hostile intent.

Helpful Guideline: Visualize your mate acting in a manner you dislike. Now visualize yourself responding to those actions more kindly. Get a clear, strong image of yourself doing that. Now, how were you able to imagine yourself responding kindly instead of with hostility? You did so by altering your attitude. You ascribed positive motives to your mate's actions (e.g., He was only trying to help) instead of negative motives.

3. *"It's not really my fault."*

Doesn't it take two to tango? Well, couples in conflict eventually believe that their spouse is the major reason marital problems persist. Women often complain that the marriage would be so much better if only he'd show more affection . . . talk about how he really feels . . . help out around the house . . . While men often complain that their wives are too critical and hard to satisfy. Each sees the other as more blameworthy.

Helpful Guideline: Once conflict is repetitious, causes and effects become interchangeable. His over involvement with work may have "caused" her to be critical, but over time her criticalness may have "caused" him to find ways to stay away from home.

Changing your counterproductive attitudes into more constructive and *realistic* attitudes, is necessary for a more satisfying marriage. Couples determined to make a success of their relationship remind themselves periodically that

- truth is relative
- their partner's negative behaviors are usually motivated by the desire for the marriage to be more satisfying
- each spouse is responsible for the current state of the relationship.

The Four Common Ways We Often Respond to Conflict

Conflict in marriage doesn't necessarily involve hostility or fighting. It occurs any time the two of you have competing needs, wants, perceptions, or desires. You want to be understood; he just can't seem to understand you. You want more romance and affection; he wants more sex. You ask him to lower his voice, he says he wasn't yelling. You say potato; he says po-tah-to . . . When in conflict you might be frightened, angry, tense, excited, depressed, or some combination of those feelings. Essentially, people in conflict are in a state of *agitation.*

Exercise: Think back a moment to a time in your childhood when you were agitated or in turmoil. Maybe your parents fought and you worried about that. Perhaps one of your school mates teased you. Did a close friend ever betray your trust or criticize you behind your back? Did somebody ever make demands upon you that made you very uncomfortable? Please don't read any further until you imagine a moment of conflict in your childhood.

Now, how did you handle the conflict? What did you do to help you reduce or get rid of the uncomfortable feelings associated with turmoil?

Because children are immature and lacking in power, they typically handle conflict in one of four ways. But consider this: *When conflict in adult life gets too uncomfortable, people often react* instinctively *and in a manner that resembles an old pattern of responding.* In short, when life gets tough, you may think you are handling conflicts maturely when in fact you are simply repeating your childhood ways of coping.

Psychologist Susan Heitler, in her textbook *From Conflict To Resolution*, discusses the four typical (but usually problematic) ways of coping with conflict:

- **Fighting:** Using force, blaming, criticizing, imposing one's will on another
- **Fleeing:** Running away, hiding, changing the topic, denying
- **Freezing:** Paralysis, procrastination, can't think straight
- **Folding:** Giving in, settling for much less, surrendering

In the exercise where I asked you to recall a moment of conflict from your childhood, which of the four ways best describes your manner of coping? Chances are good that whatever method you used as a child is the one you currently use to deal with particularly stressful situations.

A Closer Look at the Four F's

Each of the Four F's—fighting, fleeing, freezing, and folding—may be appropriate in some situations. Sometimes you have to fight and stand up for yourself, such as when you take someone to court after your rights have been violated. Sometimes you have to flee, such as when someone more powerful than you wants to harm you. Freezing-up may prevent you from making an impulsive and unwise decision, and folding (or submitting to the will of another) is appropriate when you must learn to accept a situation that cannot be changed.

Any of the Four F's becomes a problem, however, when it is used *automatically and repetitively*. When fighting or freezing-up becomes a chronic method of coping with conflict, you lack the flexibility necessary to cope adequately with a wider range of stressful events. Also, when used frequently, each of the Four F's has a tendency to *create more bad feelings*, complicating an already-difficult situation.

♥ ♥ ♥

MARRIAGE MATTERS

What *really* bothers a spouse? In a study of divorced men and women,[1] one-half of all the women said that lack of communication by their husbands (withdrawal from conversation) and lack of affection was their primary problem. One-third of women reported a lack of shared interests with their mate. Most of the divorced men believed their ex-wives did too much complaining, nagging, and fault-finding.

In terms of the Four F's then, men tend to *flee* from spending time in with their wives while women often *fight*. That finding supports other research[2] that concludes that women are more likely than men to confront their spouses with disagreements, and that men are more likely to become defensive, withdraw, or use "logic" to explain an emotional issue factually.

Repetitive use of the Four F's becomes a problem in itself. Husbands who believe their wives complain (fight) too much, may withdraw. But wives who believe their husbands withdraw too much may complain.

♥ ♥ ♥

Let's take a closer look at each of the Four F's.

Fighting

Whether you fight with rage and threatening gestures or with a mild attack (cajoling, subtle criticism, barbs, sarcasm, innuendo, refusing to cooperate, giving the "cold shoulder"), the purpose of the fighting stance is to dominate, to *win*. Fighters believe that the only way to bring about effective change is through punitive persuasion. Often they are convinced that they've tried to be reasonable and courteous in the past but to no avail, and that therefore the only way to be taken seriously is to attack. Anger is the overriding feeling.

Clues to a Fighting Stance:

- Frequent use of the words "should," "always," or "never." For example, "You should know not to interrupt me when I'm speaking. Why must you always do that?"
- Criticism and fault finding.
- Asking "Why?" when no answer would be good enough. For example, "Why do you keep spending money on things we can't afford?" (Chances are the person asking the question will not be satisfied with any answer.)
- A tendency to view the partner as critical, demanding, or stubbornly uncooperative, thereby justifying your own attacking, blaming style.
- Unwillingness to consider new information that might disconfirm a preexisting belief.
- A strong sense of injustice and entitlement.
- Discrediting a partner's comments. A tendency to make your partner wrong.
- Frequent use of provocative gestures—finger pointing, fist raising, eyeball rolling, etc.

As Psychologist Susan Heitler points out, people with a predominantly fighting stance are at risk of developing a paranoid view of situations, increasingly seeing only the bad (even when it isn't there), and finding it hard to trust their partner. Fighters are also self-critical, annoyed with their imperfections and mistakes.

What one researcher calls a "hot reactor" is the person who explodes at perceptions of hurt and disloyalty, often misreading situations entirely. "Hot reactors" are extremely sensitive to criticism and rejection and therefore overreact. When a spouse of a hot reactor acts in a way that is *ambiguous* (for example, a wife decides she wants to stay up later than usual to watch television) a hot reactor may view it as a sign of rejection. When the spouse does something that is indeed annoying (she forgets to bring home the magazine he wanted to read), a hot reactor is likely to regard her "forgetfulness" as intentional and motivated by ill-will.

Recurrent angry outbursts, however harmful, are nonetheless an attempt to resolve some ongoing conflict. But they represent a "solution" that is bound to create hard feelings and additional problems.

Fleeing

Walking out of the room when an argument starts or choosing to not raise a thorny issue for fear of getting into a fight are just two of the many ways people use *fleeing* as the prominent method of coping with conflict. Fleeing can take many forms:

- Tuning out when your mate is speaking to you
- Denying a problem exists
- Use/abuse of drugs or alcohol to numb your awareness and distract you from emotional pain
- Routine overinvolvement in any activity as a way to *avoid* dealing with other important issues
- Changing topics quickly so that no one issue can be addressed fully
- Developing physical problems that compel you to avoid interpersonal problems
- "Suffering in silence"

Like any way of coping, fleeing can be useful at times. For example, in households where physical abuse occurs, battered spouses are encouraged to leave the home and get assistance from the police or a women's shelter. But done routinely, fleeing or withdrawal does not resolve problems. It postpones some and worsens others.

People with addictions withdraw ("flee") as a standard method of coping with conflict. Jim was addicted to television, or so his wife believed. What began as a way to relax after a stressful day at the office became an automatic, unbreakable habit that interfered with his family life. While watching television, Jim was often emotionally unavailable. When his children asked for help with their homework, he'd respond, "Wait until this program is over." The kids would then turn to their mother for assistance and Jim's role in his family's life diminished.

Anna was always busy, busy, busy. Marital discord was obvious, but still it seemed more important to her to clean cabinets, wipe away dishwasher spots from glassware, and basically occupy herself with mundane chores she considered essential. Consequently, marital issues never got discussed, and her husband grew more distant as his wife remained preoccupied with minutia.

Steven Beach, in his book *Depression In Marriage,* points out that depression can arise from a breakdown in the usual day-to-day marital routines—something that occurs when partners withdraw from one another (flee). For example, couples who use withdrawal as a way to deal with their distress may no longer kiss each other good-night. They may eat together less and less often. They may arrive home from work later and sleep in separate beds. In more severe cases, one may refuse all physical contact with the other. Separation and divorce represent the ultimate withdrawal.

Rarely is withdrawal or fleeing the only dysfunctional form of coping used by distressed couples. Typically, partners who withdraw also periodically engage in brief hostile exchanges (fights) before resuming a more distant and passive stance.

Avoidance of conflict serves to bring about the very thing you wished to avoid: turmoil, and the further breakdown of your marriage.

Freezing

When faced with conflict, some people become immobile. Indications of this stance include:

- Inability to think clearly when confronted
- Fretting over and over about a worrisome issue but never doing anything to resolve it
- A feeling of anxiety that never gets eased
- Indecisiveness when action is called for
- The conviction that "I'm damned if I do and damned if I don't"
- Asking for opinions but responding "Yes, but . . ." to opinions offered

Fearing the outcome if they should do the wrong thing, some people approach conflict by procrastinating. They don't necessarily avoid the issue. In fact, they may be very focused on gathering as much data as possible to help them make a decision. Couples contemplating marital therapy may discuss the option for many months, read self-help books, and ask their physician for a referral, but stop short of actually getting therapy. They give the illusion of taking the bull by the horns and doing something constructive for their relationship, but they procrastinate—sometimes to the point of paralysis.

Folding

Harriet came to therapy because she was unhappy with her marriage. Expressing some dissatisfaction with her husband ("He never wants to go anywhere with me") she primarily criticized herself. "What's wrong with me? Something must be wrong if my husband shows no interest in me." She criticized her looks, she criticized her parenting skills, and she criticized her performance at her job. In discussing her marriage it became clear that she deferred to her husband a great deal. When he commanded, she obeyed. In an argument, he'd quickly get the upper hand by his skillful use of logic. In sum, he *dominated* and she *submitted*. Unfortunately, routine use of submission—giving in to avoid conflict—made her seriously depressed, too.

If your tendency is to *fold*, you probably:

- Walk on tiptoes to avoid arguments
- Think poorly of yourself
- Feel helpless, ineffective
- Attach yourself to someone you think has strong convictions
- Talk yourself out of activities you might enjoy by convincing yourself you "shouldn't" be selfish or you "should" take care of other's needs first.
- Appease others
- Don't stand up for yourself

About 50 percent of women who enter therapy for marriage problems are clinically depressed. Depressed people feel ineffective and overpowered by life's events. They feel as if they've had to submit again and again to forces outside of themselves.

In a marriage with a dominant-submissive pattern of relating, it is important to understand that the dominant person is not purely a controlling, demanding person. Nor is the submissive person utterly helpless. Furthermore, the more one person acts submissively, the more the other is encouraged to act in a dominant manner, and vice versa.

Vera saw Chuck as dominant and authoritative. It was his way or no way. She was passive and submissive. But often when he'd ask her opinion about something, like "Where would you like to go this weekend?" she'd respond, "It doesn't matter." So Chuck would decide for both of them. A spouse with a submissive style often defers to his or her partner, only strengthening the partner's dominating style.

If your behaving in manner "X" prompts your partner to behave in manner "Y," you can reduce the frequency with which your mate acts in manner "Y" by reducing the frequency with which you act in manner "X".

The Fifth "F": Facing the Issues in a Fair and Firm Way

Every therapist and every self-help book says the same thing when it comes to coping constructively with conflict. The issues must be *faced*, not avoided. And the couple must learn to address the issues *fairly*, without their usual "uncooperative" manners. The fight stance—blaming, criticizing, showing contempt, mistrusting—only complicates the difficulties. If you or your mate uses the fighting stance and it hasn't helped by now, it won't ever help.

If avoiding conflict by excessive use of withdrawal or by excessive overinvolvement in some form of addiction hasn't resolved your marital woes by now, what makes you think more of the same strategy will work this time?

If giving in to avoid conflict hasn't improved your attitude about the relationship, giving in one more time surely won't improve the situation.

BUILDING A SUCCESSFUL RELATIONSHIP

A 1991 study[3] examined the relationship of 662 married couples. Four tactics commonly used to keep the relationship strong were:

1. *Positiveness.* Spouses were optimistic, gave each other the benefit of the doubt, and were reluctant to find-fault.

2. *Assurances.* Spouses acted in a way that assured each other of their commitment to the marriage and their devotion to one another. Such faith in one another is difficult to maintain if fighting, withdrawal, or perceptions of being dominated permeate the relationship.

3. *Openness.* Spouses created an atmosphere of safety and a willingness to express themselves despite any discomfort in doing so. Blaming and criticizing corrode feelings of safety. Fleeing conversations is the antithesis of openness and stifles intimacy.

4. *Sharing tasks.* Spouses divided the housekeeping chores and child-rearing activities fairly. No dominant-submissive pattern operated.

Keep in Mind

- If you and your mate frequently disagree about "what really happened," arguing the "facts" won't help. Better to acknowledge what your mate says that makes sense, or validate his or her feelings (e.g., "If you really think I purposely said things to hurt you, I can't blame you for feeling angry") than to debate.

- If your partner says something hurtful and you regard his motives as malicious and as resulting from a character flaw, you won't give him the benefit of the doubt, and he'll resent you for it.

- Couples revolving on a merry-go-round of recurrent conflict don't want to fight, but they do want to be taken seriously. Sometimes arguing is their way of demonstrating their frustration over not having been heard.

- Sometimes withdrawing or submitting is the couple's way of keeping the peace, but there is no friendliness or fairness in such an arrangement.

Chapter 4

Common Patterns of Endless Arguments

Marital conflict *persists* for reasons very different from those that started the conflict in the first place. Chapter 1 showed that the way a couple *responds* to a disturbance in the relationship can paradoxically *intensify the conflict*. Frustrated by repetitive arguments and disappointments, couples in conflict dance the same dance:

- They reapply the same "solutions" and get the same unsatisfying result.
- They break the rules of effective communication yet become infuriated that their mate won't understand them.
- They withdraw in disgust from their mate precisely when he or she wants to cooperate and work things out.

Couples in conflict also sing the same tune:

- "My version of events is true, your version is false." ("I'm right, you're wrong.")
- "You do what you do just to be difficult and make matters worse. I do what I do either because you provoked me or because I'm just trying to improve matters."
- "The fault is mostly yours."

Finally, and perhaps most important of all (although it is virtually never realized by one's frustrated partner), spouses trapped in "here we go again" conflict:

- Make frequent unilateral efforts to improve the situation by *trying to stop their own unhelpful behaviors*. Unfortunately, the other spouse *is unaware of just how hard his or her partner is trying* and fails to show enough gratitude or compassion. Feeling unappreciated, the trying-hard spouse builds resentment and eventually (because he or she is human) fails to keep the negative behaviors in check. So he or she yells, complains, blames, withdraws, gives in—or does whatever it is he or she always did that irritated their mate no end. And the cycle continues.

All of these *responses* to conflict have the unfortunate consequence of *strengthening negative beliefs about one's mate and one's marriage and creating additional bad feelings,* while doing little to resolve the original problem. A downward spiral erupts, with bad feelings causing more conflict, causing "more-of-the-same" solutions, causing bad feelings . . . Conflict in the marriage has its own momentum by this point, often having little to with what first triggered it.

As tension rises and hearts lie broken, couples don't fight about what their partner says or does, they fight about what they *imagine* their partner is saying or doing.

If they don't fight, they withdraw. But they don't just withdraw from an upsetting interaction; they withdraw from (or avoid) interactions that are *potentially* upsetting.

And if they don't fight or withdraw, they submit. They give in to demands just to keep the peace, and they give in to *anticipated* demands that haven't been demanded yet.

But hope is alive and repairs are still quite possible. First, couples on a treadmill of dissatisfaction must identify their unhelpful patterns of relating, and then modify them.

His and Her Patterns

Four patterns are described below. The first two patterns—the pursuer-distancer and the fight-fight—are perhaps the most common. The last two patterns—withdraw-withdraw and fight-submit—are less common but often more serious.

Pursuer-Distancer

The most common pattern of unhelpful relating is called the "pursuer-distancer" pattern or the "fight-flee" pattern. Essentially, the pursuer (often the female) is actively engaged in cajoling, persuading, complaining, and otherwise pushing her partner to do something that partner has apparently stubbornly resisted. Often the pursuer wants more time together, more intimate conversation, or more help around the house. The distancer (often the male) is actively engaged in resistance. He withdraws, retreats, shuts down, and otherwise flees from the pursuer. He wants "room to breathe." The pattern has many steps to it:

1. She pursues for attention and affection, he withdraws.
2. Feeling worried that the relationship is too disconnected, she pursues further. Feeling worried that the relationship is too confining, he withdraws further.
3. Eventually, each pauses in place, unsure which way to turn.
4. She pursues once again but backs off quickly when he is unresponsive. She is hurt and confused.
5. If she backs away too far, he gets worried that the relationship is too disconnected and he pursues.

6. The pattern recycles, with one pursuing and one distancing and occasionally each finding a middle ground that doesn't feel quite right.

MARRIAGE MATTERS

Researcher John Gottman and colleagues at the University of Washington[1] studied couples by hooking them up to monitors (measuring pulse rate, blood pressure, etc.) and asking the couples to discuss an area of conflict. Overall, men rapidly became physiologically uptight when discussing areas of conflict with their wives. Women did not. Consequently, men looked for ways to end the conversation prematurely because they were too uncomfortable.

Men typically withdraw from conversation in many ways: by refusing to talk further ("Case closed!"), by stonewalling (remaining physically present but psychologically detached during the conversation), or by exiting the room. Wives grow weary and frustrated by this. One study[2] showed that the intensity of wive's hostility in response to husbands' withdrawal strongly predicted marital dissatisfaction. That is, the more angry the wife was with her husband's withdrawal, the more unsatisfying the marriage was.

♥ ♥ ♥

It is not unusual for the male distancer to be viewed by his wife as out of touch with his feelings, preferring logic to emotions. Ironically, his distancing is a *highly emotional response,* despite overt evidence to the contrary. It is a maneuver to *calm himself down* by maintaining a more rigid boundary between himself and his mate. Her pursuing stance is also highly emotional, but more obviously so. She wants more *togetherness* to feel better, he wants more *separateness* to feel better. She believes he won't give her the togetherness she needs, so she tries to capture as much of it as she can—even during moments when she could comfortably do without it. He believes she won't give him the amount of "space" he needs, so he tries to take as much as he can—even during moments when he could comfortably move closer. She resists backing off without a fight for fear he would then *never* satisfy her togetherness needs ("Look what I have to go through just to get him to talk with me during breakfast!" said one exasperated wife). He resists moving toward her for fear she would *never* give him space he craves.

As this pattern repeats itself, the main unproductive indicators listed at the beginning of this chapter surface:

1. Each reapplies the same "solution" to the problem, but more intensively, she continues to pursue, he to withdraw.

2. They break the rules of effective communication by failing to discuss their concerns, or by accusing and making demands (*"Why won't you talk to me?" "Just leave me alone"*).

3. When the distancer finally wants to move closer, the pursuer has "had it" and backs away. Thus, they never work in synchrony with one another.

4. Each one believes he or she knows "the truth" about the nature of the problem, and it is always something negative about his or her partner or their relationship. ("She's too needy and dependent" . . . "He's too cold and aloof" . . . "We're just incompatible.")

5. Each one secretly tries to suppress his or her own troublesome behavior. He tries to stay connected when he'd like to flee, and she tries to restrain herself from pursuing. Unfortunately, such actions are hard for the partner to notice because *not* pursuing and *not* distancing are less obvious than pursuing and distancing. Chances are, if Chuck is busy watching television and his wife Camille, who wants his company, chooses to leave him be, *he won't notice that* as quickly as he'd notice her effort to entice him away from the TV.

   And after a few days of trying hard not to push for too much togetherness, Camille will feel entitled to make some demands for more closeness and will expect Chuck to be reasonable. Now Chuck, who didn't really notice all the free time he had the past few days, views her as "not having changed," and he feels frustrated and pessimistic. Hurt and angered by this response from him, Camille shakes her head and wonders, "Can this marriage be saved?"

Solution: The real problem is not that one is too afraid of closeness or too afraid of separateness. Every person must grapple with the ongoing issue of how to remain an independent person while also remaining close to others. Most couples are somewhat out-of-sync on this issue. The real problem is the persistent effort to get one's spouse to change. That effort only increases conflict and polarizes the couple further.

1. Understand that this fight-flee problem is extremely common. The presence of this pattern alone does not signify incompatibility.

2. Understand that insisting your mate tolerate more aloneness or more togetherness is inflaming the situation.

3. Do what psychologist Daniel Wile suggests in his book *After the Honeymoon*: Inform your mate of your desire for more togetherness (or more "space") while acknowledging in a nonaccusing way that you understand your mate may have an opposite need at that moment. For example, if Camille tells Chuck, "This is one of those times I'd ordinarily push for some togetherness, but I know you sometimes have a need to be alone" then chances are Chuck would appreciate her understanding his position. Believing she is willing to give him the space he needs, he may

no longer have a need to take it. And he may be willing to spend time together with her, just as she wanted.

Fight-Fight

The late and esteemed family therapist Virginia Satir once said, "When we abuse each other, what we are doing is saying we are starving to death and will do cannibalism in order to live."

Couples who routinely fight and blame do seem to be tearing down the structure they are ostensibly fighting to protect. Many marriages run by fighters survive, but the marriage isn't all that satisfying.

Of course, couples with a fight-fight pattern will also withdraw from time to time. And often they will strain themselves not to argue when they really feel like arguing, which is part of their problem too. Like Chuck and Camille in the fight-flee pattern, members of a fight-fight couple won't always notice when the other spouse is trying to bite his tongue and restrain himself from doing something provocative. (Once again, it is more difficult to notice the *absence* of a particular behavior.) And if the first spouse does notice, she will quickly be dismayed the next time her partner reverts to his usual style. She will then accuse her mate of "not trying hard enough," prompting the reply, "I *was* trying but you didn't seem to care." At that point, the argument deteriorates into debates over who was trying harder and caring more. Eventually, one or both will withdraw in disgust.

Commonly, fight-fight couples:

- Continue to push their partners' buttons. The main reason they do this is that they are very hurt and angry and don't think their mate cares. So they attack, partly out of vengeance and partly to coerce their partner to take them more seriously. Of course, coercive efforts only hurt the other spouse more, leading her to attack in return, partly out of vengeance and partly to coerce her mate to take her more seriously. Once in a while, intense anger does result in getting your spouse to take you more seriously. *Is this what I have to go through just to get my spouse to understand and care about me?* one wonders in dismay.

- Argue in an "I'm right, you're wrong" manner over issues that have no clear right or wrong answer. Phil and Liz debated how to open Christmas presents. He believed families should wait until Christmas morning to open gifts, and that everybody should open their presents at the same time. She preferred that everybody take turns, opening one gift at a time so that others could watch the expression on the face of the recipient, and why wait until Christmas morning when Christmas Eve is better!

- Fight over semantics or some other side issue and ignore the spirit of what's being discussed.

  He: "I saw you staring at that man over there."
  She: "I wasn't *staring*, I was just *looking*."
  He: "Do you expect me to believe that?"
  She: "I don't expect anything. I just wish you'd stop picking at everything I do."
  He: "Just answer me this: Do you or do you not think that man over there is attractive?"
  She: "I don't have to answer that!"
  He: "I'm asking a simple question. Why won't you answer it?"
  She: "Doesn't a woman have a right to *look* at another man?"
  He: "You're still not answering the question. And besides, you didn't *look*, you *stared*."

  He wanted some reassurances from his wife that she was committed to the relationship, but his implied accusation that she was interested in other men irritated her. She was then unable to offer reassurances. Arguing whether she "looked" or "stared," or debating whether or not a woman has a right to look at another man, diverted them from the spirit of the issue.

- Say and do many more hurtful things than they remember saying and doing. One reason for this is that their anger leaks out at a time when they are trying to keep it in check. So they don't realize that their tone of voice, body posture, or facial gesture conveys hostility. Bob was fiddling with the VCR, which wasn't working properly. His wife Amanda, who'd been trying to keep her anger in check, said in a gruff tone, "What are you trying to do?" He heard her hostility and believed she was criticizing him, so he shot back, "What does it look like I'm doing?" She walked away in a huff wondering why he couldn't respond matter-of-factly to a simple question.

  Accusing a spouse of being hostile, mean-spirited, loud, rude, or critical won't help if it hasn't helped before. A good response: *"It hurts (or concerns me) when I think you're being critical."* That puts the emphasis on your response, not on his or her actions.

Some fight-fight couples can find themselves in explosive situations. See "Building a Successful Relationship" for advice.

BUILDING A SUCCESSFUL RELATIONSHIP

How best to defuse an explosive situation? If a spouse is angry, it is probably because he or she hasn't felt heard or understood, or because he or she felt attacked, unfairly blamed, or criticized.

What To Do

1. Any response, however justified, that conveys an attitude of "You're wrong to feel angry" will fuel the explosion. Instead, *validate* what makes sense about the other's anger: e.g., "I don't blame you for being angry . . ." Feeling understood, the person may start to calm down. Simply saying in a clear, respectful voice "I hear your anger" also can help the person feel heard.

2. Apologize if the explosiveness is in response to something you said or did that was hurtful. If you aren't sure what you said or did that prompted the outburst, ask.

3. Psychologist Susan Heitler advises that when anger has escalated to a potentially dangerous degree, yelling "Stop! That's enough! We'll talk again later" may be necessary. Leaving the situation may also be necessary.

4. If you and your mate have had explosive outbursts but are working to halt them, a firm reminder by the calmer spouse that "It's getting out of hand. Let's back up and try again" is useful.

♥ ♥ ♥

Solution:

1. Fight-fight couples should draw up a list of unacceptable behaviors during an argument (for example, It is unacceptable for you to swear at me . . . It is unacceptable for you to interrupt me, etc.). Common elements of such a list include: no shouting, no physically intimidating gestures, no taking phone calls. Once listed, each must agree to follow the guidelines set down.

2. Spouses should remain seated while discussing an area of conflict. Standing up is associated with greater frequency of abuse, shouting, and premature exits.

3. Spouses should agree to speak in a quieter-than-normal tone of voice. Research indicates that a speaker's anger intensifies when she is talking loudly and diminishes when she speaks softly.

4. Until each has greater confidence in problem-solving skills, discussions should be time-limited, with the promise to resume the discussion later at a preagreed time. The length of time to set aside for a discussion is different for each couple. Rule of thumb: Start small and work your way to longer time periods.

Withdraw-Withdraw

As in the purser-distancer and the fight-fight patterns, couples in this pattern will periodically fight. Usually, however, major skirmishes occur only once in a while, since the preferred mode of dealing with conflict is to *flee.*

It is the manner of fleeing that determines the substance of this marital arrangement. Partners with no mutual interests and hectic lives may become the proverbial "ships passing in the night." Neither one may feel good about the relationship, but they won't discuss it. Marriages with this pattern have a higher risk of infidelity.

More commonly, each spouse flees by overinvolving him-or herself in some addiction. One spouse may drink too much, the other may work too much or spend too much. If they argue, it may be about spending habits or alcoholism.

This pattern can be difficult to break once an addictive process gets underway. Marital dissatisfaction reinforces addictiveness, which then adds to marital dissatisfaction.

Solution: If a serious addiction is present, it must treated. Marriage therapy will also be helpful. If no addiction is present, it is essential to realize that avoidance of conflict (via withdrawal) has long-term disastrous consequences. The couple needs to learn effective communication skills and be willing to tolerate the anxiety that accompanies dialogue.

Fight-Submit

This pattern has two forms: a dominant-submissive form or an overfunctioner-underfunctioner form. In the dominant-submissive form, one spouse routinely gives in to the wishes and demands of the other. Often the submissive partner fears conflict. Over time, the submissive partner is at high risk for becoming clinically depressed. Indications of depression include loss of interest in sex and other pleasurable activities, sleep and appetite disturbance, crying spells, and pessimism about oneself, one's situation, and the future. Submissive spouses often feel a great deal of guilt.

The domineering spouse (often, but not always, the man) may not be harsh. He may simply be someone with a tendency to want to control matters. The more his wife submits, the more he takes over (which makes her even more passive and submissive).

Many submissive wives and domineering husbands may be repeating a pattern from their childhood or previous marriage. Typically their fathers were domineering, hard to satisfy, or abusive. As the submissive wife starts to assert herself, the domineering husband will protest (the longer the fight-submit pattern was in place, the more intensely the husband will protest). Both partners have low self-esteem; she because she views herself as helpless, and he because he needs his partner to be submissive in order to feel okay about himself. Thus, as the wife asserts herself, the husband will feel threatened and will act in ways to regain his dominant position.

Betty and Bob fit the overfunctioner-underfunctioner pattern. Bob had gone through a series of unsatisfying jobs and at age thirty-five still hadn't quite found himself. To complicate matters, he developed symptoms of fatigue and joint pain that left the physicians stymied. Eventually, he was diagnosed with Chronic Fatigue Syndrome, but some doctors weren't so sure. Betty was energetic and able to keep her successful job as a real-estate broker. She sometimes worked seven days a week, kept the house clean, bought groceries, and was always at Bob's side when he needed comfort and reassurance. This pattern continued for several years. They came to therapy because Betty was becoming "burned out" and she wanted assistance to get her back to her former level of functioning. In sessions, Betty showed clear signs of being an overfunctioner:

1. She talked more than she listened
2. She offered Bob assistance before it was even clear that he might require assistance ("I'll help you unpack the groceries, Bob" or "Bob, why don't you let me type up your resume").
3. She felt guilty and responsible when Bob wasn't feeling up to some project.

Bob showed clear signs of being an underfunctioner:

1. He let Betty do most of the talking.
2. He deferred to her for decisions he could easily make.
3. His future goals were vague. Any decisions he did make he had difficulty following through on.

On the surface it seems that Betty is healthy—amazingly able to function over the years despite her burdens—and that Bob is the unhealthy one. But when this pattern persists for years, the truth is that neither one is as emotionally healthy as it would appear. Betty has lost sight of herself. She's overtired but ignores that fact until she physically and emotionally "burns out." She worries about her husband but doesn't take care of her needs. By overfunctioning, she has enabled Bob to underfunction. For emotional healing to occur, Betty needs to focus more on her needs and less on Bob's. That will result in short-term distress for Bob (chances are his Chronic Fatigue will act up) and distress for Betty as she feels guilty. But if she can hang in there, Bob will be forced to do more for himself.

Solution: Ultimately, the relationship must become more equitable. The main stumbling block is the motivation of the partners to continue making progress. In the dominant-submissive pattern, the dominant spouse is afraid of losing control over the marriage, while the submissive spouse lacks a strong sense of conviction to assert herself routinely. Ironically, from the standpoint of power, depressed and helpless individuals can wield great power in a family by requiring others to do things for them. (When an infant cries in the middle of the night and needs to be fed, one can legitimately ask the question, "Who's in charge? The parent or the child?")

In the overfunctioning-underfunctioning pattern, the overfunctioner must learn to be more selfish—taking care of his or her needs first. It will seem heartless and cruel and will result in a worsening of the underfunctioner's symptoms at first, but no other solution will work.

Since it can be a bit frightening for couples who wish to change this pattern, it is helpful to increase demonstrations of caring, attention, and tenderness. Fearing rejection and feeling inadequate, partners need to know they are cared for and that their mate is still committed to the relationship.

One Last Important Thing You Need to Know

When a relationship problem has persisted for over six months, or if numerous problems have cropped up over that time, conflict has become *chronic*. Although it seems logical to presume that the longer a problem has gone unresolved, the happier the partners will be when it is resolved, the opposite is usually true. *Precisely when progress has been made, at least one partner will show anger or pessimism.* Most often the anger stems from disillusionment that it took them so long to improve matters. They wonder whether it's worth being in a relationship where problems can't be solved sooner. Sometimes the anger is a sign that some important issue has remained hidden and needs to be addressed. When improvements have been made, it is a tactical error to respond to a spouse's unexpected anger with criticism or a "Why do I even bother to try" attitude. Inquiring what the anger is about and determining whether your spouse has any unstated concerns about the relationship is a better approach.

Keep in Mind

- Why a problem *persists* is more important to understand than why a problem started. Problems persist because "solutions" that previously failed are not abandoned but applied more strenuously, intensifying misunderstandings and hurt feelings.

- Reducing obnoxious or hurtful behaviors is essential for a healthy marriage. However, it is not as easy for a partner to notice the *absence* of a behavior. Adding positive behaviors to one's repertoire is more noticeable than subtracting negative behaviors.

- Patterns such as Pursue-Distance, Overfunction-Underfunction, Dominate-Submit, and Fight-Fight are sustained by the reinforcing effects of each partner's position. The more one pursues, the more the other will distance, causing more pursuit, and so forth.

- Remaining seated during an argument may keep you both calmer and prevent explosive outbursts.

- Speaking in a loud tone of voice *increases* the anger of the speaker. Speaking in a quieter-than-normal voice reduces anger.

- Don't be surprised if the reaction to a positive change in the relationship is anger, irritation, or lack of appreciation. The longer a problem persisted, the more bad feelings developed. Those bad feelings won't disappear immediately simply because the relationship has taken a turn for the better.

Chapter 5

The First Step to Halting Recurrent Conflict: Unhooking Emotional Triangles

It is difficult to do marriage therapy with only one of the spouses. One reason is that no matter how hard the therapist tries to be objective, he or she has an increased chance of developing a bias against one of the spouses (usually the absent spouse, who is most often the husband). If the wife complains to her therapist on a weekly basis about just how awful her marriage is and how unfeeling her husband is, chances are the wife will come out of a session feeling *relief*—not because her marriage is improving, but because she feels supported in her belief that her husband is primarily to blame for their problems.

When that happens, therapy may be an obstacle to marital improvement.

In the example just given, an *emotional triangle* was formed. Emotional triangles occur in most relationships, and they have the effect of *perpetuating the status quo*, not introducing change. An emotional triangle can occur any time the tension between any two people gets too high. One of the spouses will bring in a third party either to complain to about his or her partner, or to divert attention from the marriage. The result is a slight lessening of tension between the married partners and an increase in anxiety in the third person. A therapist who feel frustrated or uptight conducting marital therapy with only one of the spouses is probably caught in an emotional triangle.

Pat and Mike were unhappy, and no effort to improve matters had helped. So Pat complained to her mother about Mike. Pat received support from her mother, who, over time, began to believe that her son-in-law was behaving irresponsibly. Pat's anxiety lessened as she felt understood by her mother, while the mother's stress level rose accordingly. Meanwhile, although Mike was annoyed at Pat's daily phone calls to her Mom, he was relieved that he and Pat had stopped trying to talk about their problems—talking had never helped, anyway. The triangle, formed originally as a maneuver to reduce tension, had effectively prevented future success at resolving problems. Pat and her Mom were convinced that Mike needed to do all the changing, so Pat was reluctant to put forth much effort anymore. Mike felt ganged up on and didn't think his mother-in-law knew "the whole story," so he dug his heels in deeper, unwilling to cooperate.

In every triangle, two people are aligned against the third. In Pat and Mike's case, Pat and her Mom were united while Mike was on the outside. But then an interesting thing happened, something that arises frequently in emotional triangles: A shift occurred. Pat's Mom became increasingly angry at Mike and began berating him face-to-face. Pat, while somewhat happy to see Mike "getting what he deserved," was taken aback by the intensity of her Mom's anger. So she politely but firmly advised her Mom to "back off—it's between me and Mike," while disagreeing about a point her Mom had just made—effectively coming to Mike's rescue and discrediting her mother's role.

"Mom, Mike doesn't drink *that* much."

"I thought you told me he went to the bars regularly after work," Mom shot back.

"Well, once in a while he does. But he's been coming home on time lately."

With this slight shift, Pat and Mike have aligned themselves more closely and now Mom is more on the outside. Taking this a bit further, let's imagine that now Mike agrees to attend therapy sessions with Pat and their marriage does start to improve. Let's also imagine (it's not hard) that once in a while Pat complains mildly about Mike to her Mom, who still can't quite forgive her son-in-law. As time goes on, Pat can't talk with her Mom without the mother criticizing Mike. Pat must then come to Mike's defense, and she gets angry with her mother for fueling conflict at a time when Pat and Mike are trying to work things out. Now tension is high between Pat and her Mom, but lower between Pat and Mike. To add to the situation, let's imagine that Pat's father is fed up with his wife's "interfering" in his daughter's marriage. He's also fed up with his daughter's being harsh to her mother, especially after all the time the mother has spent trying to help Pat with her marriage. So he orders his wife to "stay out of it" and he orders his daughter to "apologize to your mother." Both women get infuriated at him. Disgusted, Dad invites Mike out to the bar for a drink to commiserate about how emotionally oversensitive women are.

It's no wonder some problems can't get resolved.

Six Kinds of Triangles

In the typical marriage, the most common triangles are the *in-law triangle,* where an in-law somehow gets in the middle between a bickering couple; the *child triangle,* where a child distracts a couple from focusing on the marriage; the *stepfamily triangle,* where the loyalties of one parent are divided between her spouse and her biological children; the *symptom triangle,* where a physical or emotional symptom flares up at a time when a couple might otherwise be focusing on their relationship; the *workplace triangle,* where one spouse overinvolves himself in his job as a way to avoid marital issues; and the *affair triangle,* where one partner has an affair as a way to contend with marital dissatisfaction. Once again, triangles lower anxiety at first, as they enable one or both spouses to *flee* or *withdraw* from dealing with the marriage, but perpetuate anxiety in the long run, since problems are successfully avoided but not successfully resolved.

In triangles involving a third person, that person is "triangled in" by one of two methods: either he is drawn into the fray by one of the other two, or he *voluntarily* enters the scene after witnessing conflict between the two.

The In-Law Triangle

When Pat and Mike had marital problems, Pat "triangled in" her mother by complaining to her about Mike. Eventually Pat didn't need to seek her mother out, because her mother would call Pat on the phone or criticize Mike without specifically being asked. Often Pat spent more time complaining to her Mom *about* Mike than she ever spent talking *with* Mike.

The most common in-law triangle occurs when one parent can't get along with his or her son-or daughter-in-law. This is usually not prompted by a marital problem but by some longstanding issue between the parent and adult child. A mother and daughter who have some unresolved issue between them may find themselves in a situation where the mother is in conflict with her son-in-law. The solution to that triangle is for Mom and daughter to put the cards on the table and work matters out between them instead of displacing the anger on to the son-in-law.

In-law triangles also complicate matters because they often get misidentified as signs of family *loyalty.* A wife who spends more time with her parents because she is unhappy in her marriage may view what she's doing as natural and an indication of "just how close I am to my parents." Her parents, too, may regard it as their role to intervene if their daughter is unhappy since "that's what caring parents do." Disconnecting such a triangle is difficult if the triangle is desired and viewed as healthy.

The Child Triangle

Sometimes the third person *distracts* the couple from their conflict, as when an unhappy couple must concentrate on a child's serious school problem and less on their marital problems. If the school problem persists, the couple may blame one another ("Our son wouldn't be failing reading if you had spent more time with him"), which may add to their resentment. However, the focus on the child can also operate to prevent the couple from "having it out," placing the marriage in grave jeopardy. Either way the status quo persists, which is what triangles accomplish.

Sometimes a child (or relative or friend) may form the third side of a triangle because the couple "unwittingly" argued within earshot of the child. Or the child may purposely intrude on a bickering couple as a mediator (if the child is older) or as a distraction (if the child is younger). Many children are not aware of their role as distractor and may not act up for the purpose of getting their parents to focus on them instead of their marriage. It might be that as a couple starts to argue, a child will accidentally spill a glass of milk or ask an irrelevant question. But the effect is the same: When a child succeeds in becoming the third leg in a triangle with his parents, he or she runs a risk of developing symptoms (physical or emotional) that will further keep the attention away from the marriage. *If the child's symptoms serve the purpose of keeping a married couple from fighting (or interrupting them) or delaying them from ending their marriage, the child's symptoms may not disappear with straightforward, "common-sense" treatment* (such as providing a tutor to a child with poor grades).

Child-focused triangles are sometimes difficult to identify, since a child problem is a natural focus for parents. Parents must be honest with themselves in determining whether they focus on the child's problems precisely at a time they might otherwise be focusing on the marriage relationship. If so, a child-focused triangle has developed.

The Stepfamily Triangle

With the divorce rate steady at 50 percent, and remarriage a likely choice for most people, many children will be raised by a stepparent at some point during their childhood. (Incidentally, the odds that a child born today will experience a *second* parental divorce before the age of eighteen is 40 percent.) Stepfamilies come with their own set of problems. If the children are over the age of seven, they may not accept the stepparent as a legitimate parent. The stepparent is in the unenviable position of trying to be a co-leader in a family where all of its members may not accept his or her authority. The natural parent often feels torn—wanting to soothe any hurts the children may have from the divorce, but not wanting to allow the children to be continuously disrespectful to the stepparent. Sticking up for the kids looks like siding against the new spouse, and vice versa. As tension between the stepparent and children rises, the biological parent may step in and try to calm things down. If this is done routinely, the stepparent and child may never learn to resolve issues on their own or develop a one-to-one relationship.

The Symptom Triangle

This forms when one of the spouses develops (or pays attention to) physical or emotional symptoms as a way to divert attention from a troubled marriage. For example, Joan Atwood, a marriage and family counselor at Hofstra University, reported that premenstrual mood changes affected the personal relationships of 45 percent of the women she studied. In some cases, husbands discredited their wives' complaints about the relationship by saying, "She's PMS-ing." Some women allowed themselves to vent anger during their menstrual period by telling themselves, "It's not me, it's my PMS." In such cases, the presence of PMS symptoms became a third leg in an emotional triangle, allowing spouses to avoid dealing with their marital issues honestly and straightforwardly. Backaches, migraines, ulcers, depression, anxiety, obesity, or any other chronic condition may unwittingly be emphasized or focused on as a way to distract a person from marital issues. The old cliché "Not tonight, I have a headache" should be a warning that any real symptom that eventually serves the purpose of keeping the person distracted from some other important (but scary) area of life may never go away.

The Workplace Triangle

People who avoid dealing with the marriage by working late or volunteering for overtime perpetuate the marital problems. Working late reduces relationship anxiety in the short run but maintains the anxiety over the long haul because the marital issues never get resolved. Instead they get *reshelved.*

Similar to the child triangle, the workplace triangle is sometimes difficult to identify because "legitimate" reasons can be made why a spouse must work more hours. The need for additional money or the need to advance one's career may mask a more important reason: If one didn't work late, one would have to spend more time with one's spouse—something unhappy couples are reluctant to do.

The Affair Triangle

A "love triangle," commonly referred to as an "affair," more obviously perpetuates marital problems—even though the affair was a temporary "solution" for at least one of the partners. Let's say a woman is unhappy in her marriage and has an affair. She has no intention of divorcing her husband or marrying the other man, yet every time she's upset with her mate, instead of trying to work things out, she sees her lover. Feeling rejuvenated, she tolerates some of her husband's faults and fights with him less often, knowing she always has her lover to turn to when she needs him. Thus, although the marriage doesn't improve, day-to-day tensions and arguments have probably declined (until the husband finds out about the affair . . .) One couple had numerous relationship problems, including the husband's low sexual desire and periodic erectile failures. His wife wanted him to see a doctor, but he refused. Their arguments about that virtually halted after she began a fling with a man from the office. Her affair reduced conflict at home but did nothing to improve the marital situation.

It is usually unwise for a couple to participate in marital therapy if one spouse is having an affair and does not intend to halt it. This is because the affair is not merely a *consequence* of a troubled marriage, it is now the *cause* of further problems. If a husband is having an affair, the likelihood is that he and his wife will continue to experience misunderstandings and other difficulties even as they are trying to improve their relationship. But if he sees the "other woman" while he and his wife are trying to work things out, the other woman will inevitably be more understanding, patient, consoling, and passionate than his wife could be (given the circumstances of their marriage)—which will only diminish his wife in the man's eyes.

BUILDING A SUCCESSFUL RELATIONSHIP

There is a seventh kind of triangle that is very common but quite hidden. In their book *The Evaluation and Treatment of Marital Conflict*, psychologist Philip Guerin and colleagues discuss "the fantasy solution." The fantasy solution is one spouse's idealized answer to an ongoing marital problem. That spouse might fantasize about some imaginary lover. Or he or she might fantasize about divorce, or about living alone, or even about being widowed. This fantasy becomes the third leg in a triangle when the spouse routinely retreats to the fantasy instead of dealing with the real-life marital concerns. Someone with a fantasy solution spends a great amount of time imagining about it. Rather than motivating the person to improve the marriage, the fantasy moves the person away from the marriage emotionally, and reducing his desire to examine his own role in the marital problems.

If your fantasy solutions have formed a wedge between you and your mate, you must first understand that your fantasy is no longer "harmless." Even if you never act on it, retreating to it over and over can keep you from addressing legitimate marital concerns, just as daydreaming can keep an employee from completing her job assignment. Still, dealing squarely with your marriage problems may be difficult, too. Your best bet is to view your fantasy as a cue that you are avoiding some marital issue, and use that as a sign that you need to talk with your mate. If he won't talk, or if no constructive dialogue unfolds, consider seeing a qualified marriage therapist. Even a handful of sessions can work wonders for a motivated couple.

♥ ♥ ♥

Clues to Emotional Triangles

Please bear in mind that . . .

- . . . the presence of in-laws in your daily life does not automatically mean an in-law triangle exists

- . . . physical, social, or emotional problems in a child do not automatically mean a child-focused triangle exists

- . . . the presence of chronic physical or emotional symptoms in you or your mate does not automatically mean that a symptom-focused triangle exist

- . . . having a stepfamily does not automatically mean that stepfamily triangles exist

- ... working extra hours does not automatically mean a workplace-focused triangle exists

A marriage triangle exists only when one spouse focuses on a child, parent, a job, or a symptom *in order to divert attention away from something in the marital relationship*. To make a triangle complete, that third person must be willing to get "in the middle" (or be unable to get out of the middle). A triangle persists only with the willing involvement of all three people in the triangle.

You may be in a triangle and not know it. One reason triangles persist, in fact, is that participants are unaware of what's happening. Or if they are aware, some participants believe they are doing the right thing. A parent who sides with a son against a daughter-in-law may feel he is being loyal to his son. An adult daughter who routinely listens to her mother complain about her father may honestly be wishing to provide support and help heal a troubled relationship. In these cases, efforts to remove oneself from a triangle may generate anxiety or guilt, the belief that one is abandoning a loved one or not being a "good enough" child. The issue is not really one of loyalty, although it can feel that way. But if your presence is *preventing* two others from working things out, you may not be helping at all.

Clues to possible triangles include:

- Marital disagreements that recycle and never get resolved.
- Periodically finding yourself "in the middle" of conflict between two others (such as your spouse and your child; your mother and your father; your spouse and his job; your spouse and your parent).
- The presence of a "black sheep" in your family. ("Black sheep" may sometimes be focused on by others in order for them to *divert* attention from other legitimate family problems.)
- Gossip. Complaining about somebody else the person is not present reveals unsettled relationship issues.
- Feeling responsible for someone else's feelings. If this is happening to you, you may jump in and try to solve the person's problems for her, thereby becoming the middleman.
- The "If it's not one thing, it's another" syndrome. When families are bothered by numerous "one right after the other" problems, it suggests that a more fundamental problem (perhaps the marriage relationship) has not been adequately resolved. By having to focus on the numerous other problems, the couple never get to address the marriage issues. (It is also possible that because of increased stress and low tolerance for frustration, "normal" family problems that ordinarily would be handled well are mishandled—giving the impression that the family is being mysteriously besieged by numerous problems.)

- The presence of chronic anxiety in at least one family member. Triangles form because anxiety is too high and unmanageable. Triangles redistribute anxiety so that one person or two people don't carry the full load.

- Depression in one marital partner. The likelihood that a depressed spouse has marital problems is 50 percent. A spouse with marital concerns is not likely to develop depression unless a feeling of hopelessness and helplessness has set in. Since triangles perpetuate the status quo and prevent change, a spouse may be caught in a triangle and unable to resolve marital problems, thereby increasing a feeling of helplessness.

Three's a Crowd: How to Unhook Yourself from Emotional Triangles

First of all, don't expect to unhook yourself from every triangle in your life. Emotional triangles are omnipresent, and like many negative things (such as physical pain) they serve a protective purpose. (Without experiencing physical pain, we might persist in doing something that could seriously harm us.)

While triangles often prevent change for the better, they frequently keep matters from getting much worse. A couple involved in a child-focused triangle may not improve their marital satisfaction, but they may avoid dealing with some issues that, if not resolved delicately, could result in the dissolution of the marriage. Remember the woman who had an affair to help her cope with her husband's low sexual desire? Her affair kept the couple from arguing about his sexual difficulties. The marriage did not improve, but the cease-fire on the home front certainly was a relief. (An analogy: Imagine an employee who is dissatisfied with his boss but is afraid to speak to the boss, fearing the boss "would take it the wrong way" and make life more difficult for him. Instead, the employee complains regularly to his coworkers about his boss, thereby getting some relief and understanding. However, his job satisfaction never improves. "But at least I still have a job," he tells himself.)

So be forewarned: Since the function of triangles is to lower anxiety by redistributing it, any effort to unhook yourself from a triangle will *temporarily raise the anxiety in the three-person system.* In other words, you'll feel like you've made a mistake. And if you are the middleman in the triangle, you may even be accused of being insensitive to the needs of others. Actually, *if your efforts to get out of a triangle do not cause an increase in anxiety (in at least one of the other two people), then you have not successfully unhooked yourself.*

Once in a while it is easy to unhook yourself from a triangle. Once Jane and Al realized that they avoided their relationship issues by occupying themselves with busywork (tidying the house, making sure all dishes were cleared and the counter was spotless, etc.), they agreed to spend fifteen minutes a night being together—often they took an evening stroll around their block.

But triangles are stubborn things and usually require a bit more than willpower to dismantle them.

Typically, four steps are necessary to detach yourself successfully from an emotional triangle.

1. You must *Pinpoint* the triangle(s) you are in.
2. You must *Plan* how you'll unhook yourself.
3. You must *Predict* how your spouse and others will react.
4. You must *Persevere* in the face of pressure to return to the triangle.

Pinpoint

This may or not be a simple step. If you feel caught in the middle between two others (say, your spouse and your child), you are probably all too aware of that triangle. Since the person in the middle is on the receiving end of anxiety that the other two distribute, the middle position is the most noticeable. So if your spouse says, "I'm grounding our son because he didn't come home on time yesterday. And I already told him you won't take him to the football game as you planned," you know you are being triangled.

However, triangles often shift in such a way that participants take turns being in the middle or being the focus of the others' anger. A mother caught in the middle between her bickering husband and son may periodically side with the husband against the son (husband-wife aligned, son on the outside), or side with the son against the husband (mother-son aligned, husband on the outside). On occasion, her husband and son may get along fine but find fault with the mother (father-son aligned, mother on the outside).

Less noticeable are the triangles formed when you and another aren't getting along and one of you pulls in a third person. Maybe you and your mother don't get along, so you pull in your spouse to align with you against your mother. Or maybe you and your spouse aren't getting along so one of you focuses on work to avoid the marital tension. Many triangles are formed less by words than by nonverbal signals. Tones of voice, gestures, and sighs can all pull you in to a triangle without there ever being an open invitation.

Your best bet is to assume the role of detached observer to your own family interactions. Watch when tension rises between two others and observe whether they triangle in another person. Or notice when you are tense with your spouse or child and observe how that tension eases. Does one of you focus on an irrelevant topic? Do you argue but halt the fight when the kids intrude or when one of you has a flare-up of some symptom?

Plan

Essentially you must accomplish three things in any plan. **First, you must** *take an "I" position* **in your communications with others.** That is, you must state what you want, don't want, will tolerate, won't tolerate, need, or don't need. Telling the others what *they* should do (taking a "you" position) keeps you tangled in the triangle. Your focus can only be on yourself, since it is easiest to change your behavior—and even that can be difficult! It should not be on changing the others in the triangle. In fact, *any persistent effort to get the other two to change (without taking an "I" focus) is an indication that the triangle is as strong as ever.*

Examples of a "you" focus:

> *"Mom, please don't complain to me about Dad."* (Here, the woman is caught in the middle between her warring parents. She has made the same request before, to no avail.)
>
> *"Why won't you quit working so much overtime and spend more time with the family?"* (Here, the woman is in a triangle with her husband and his workplace.)

Examples of an "I" focus:

> *"Mom, I will have to hang up if you keep complaining about Dad."*
>
> *"Your work involvement worries me, since we rarely see you anymore. I'm unhappy and want to talk with you about how I can feel better."*

Second, you must *remain in contact with the others* **at the same time you are trying to disconnect the triangle.** People often mistakenly believe that by cutting themselves off from others they can extricate themselves from a triangle. Not so. Your physical presence is irrelevant to the life of a triangle. The key is to remain in emotional contact (caring *about* them, for instance) but still remaining emotionally separate (not caring *for* them). You may touch them but not carry them. Speak to them but don't lecture. Listen, but end the conversation when they expect you to get involved in a way that only complicates your life or adds to your stress.

Third, you must *lower your emotional reactivity* **to the antics of the other two.** Just because person A is upset and person B is upset does not mean you must therefore be upset. It can matter to you that A and B have troubles, but if you get uptight because of their troubles, you run the risk of getting hooked in a triangle. If your immediate knee-jerk reaction is to "solve" the problems between A and B, or "keep the peace," or "insist" that someone act in a certain manner, or run away—you are hooked. If you require others to calm down or be happy in order for you to calm down or be happy, you are hooked. If A is hungry and B is hungry, must it automatically mean that you too must eat? If A has an itchy nose, must you sneeze? Of course not.

THE BUS DRIVER TRIANGLE

Insisting that others change (without making the effort to change yourself) is illustrated by the following scenario.

Imagine a new bus driver who is in conflict with a stern, demanding boss. The boss demands that the driver always be on time at his scheduled bus stops. So the new driver is uptight when he arrives at his bus stop. He sees a person in the distance running toward the bus, signaling him to wait. He waits, and two minutes later the person boards. Imagine that the next day the same thing happens but that this time the driver has to wait five minutes for the tardy traveler to board the bus. The driver lectures the person and threatens to leave without him next time. But the passenger is late again the following day, and the driver's ulcer starts to act up.

What should the driver have done? Though it was kind of him to wait on the first day, he would have been less anxious if he had departed on time the following days. If the passenger missed the bus because of his own tardiness, so be it. If the driver continues to "insist" that the passenger be on time while not doing anything about his own behavior (departing without waiting for the passenger), one might conclude that he, not the passenger, is to blame for his developing ulcer.

Many people stuck in family triangles act like the bus driver. They are tense and miserable and insist that others change so that they can feel better. They'd be better off changing their own behavior so that they are less dependent upon others for their happiness.

It is also necessary not to pass judgment on either A's or B's behavior as a way to lower your emotional reactivity. (That does not mean you cannot take a stand. If you find A's behavior offensive, you have a right to feel that way. But your focus needs to be on what you will do or not do in response to A, not on what person A should do or not do.) You may choose never to act in the same manner as person A, but you run the risk of being triangled when you take sides or try to determine who is to blame. It may look as if A is wrong and B is right, but chances are next time A will be right and B will be wrong and still they'll keep fighting. Your efforts to fix blame will solve nothing, *heighten* your emotional reactivity, and keep you stuck.

Want to lower your anxiety quickly? See "Marriage Matters" on the following page for some tips.

Predict

Once you've planned what you will say and do, it is best to predict how others will react to your efforts to de-triangle. Certainly it will raise their anxiety level somewhat. But what will they say and do? Will they criticize you? Will they repeat their complaints like a broken record in the hope that you will finally "do something" to help them? Will they "suffer in silence"? If you decide not to focus on the children when you and your mate are attempting to focus on your marriage, how will your mate respond? Will he try to focus on the children instead? How will you handle that? The more prepared you are for the possible reactions of others, the less anxious you will be. The lower your anxiety, the more likely you will be to succeed in your effort to detriangle. A common reaction to your detriangling efforts is to accuse you of disloyalty. If you then try to explain and justify your position, you are hooked. Remember, you don't have to explain. You don't have to justify. When you are hungry, you don't have to justify it—it's simply how you feel. When you are tired or sexually aroused, it's the same thing: No justification is necessary. Likewise, if you are taking care of your emotional needs by detaching from a triangle, you need not explain yourself.

♥ ♥ ♥
MARRIAGE MATTERS
You can lower your anxiety level immediately simply by using your diaphragm to help you breathe. Diaphragmatic breathing occurs when your stomach puffs out as you inhale. When anxious, people often breathe through their upper chests which causes them to breathe more shallowly and rapidly—a consequence that adds to the sensation of anxiety. In contrast, deep breathing slows respiration and heart rate and relaxes you.

Also, speak *slowly and softly* when communicating to the others in the triangle. Research shows that people feel more anger when they speak loudly—significantly less anger when they speak slowly and softly.

Finally, it helps to remain in a seated position when talking. Standing up increases the risk of emotional flare-ups.

♥ ♥ ♥

Persevere

Hang in there. People prefer the status quo to change, even when the status quo hurts. If your efforts to unhook yourself succeed, others will become anxious and will pressure you to go back to your old ways. If you get agitated and furious at them because of that again, you are hooked. If others try to put you back "in the middle," your best bet is to say or do things that will prompt the other two to work it out between them. "That sounds like a matter for you and Dad to discuss, Mom. Talk to him, please, not me." They may refuse to work it out between them, but you can refuse to be the middleman. Be polite but be firm. Make no excuses. You can do it.

Keep in Mind

- If you try to unhook yourself from a triangle, anxiety will increase in the system. Be prepared.
- Make changes only for yourself. Don't try to change the other person.

- If you see villains and victims in the triangle, you are hooked.
- If you take sides in an effort to get somebody to change, you are hooked.
- If you routinely try to solve the problems of others, keep the peace, assume responsibility for the feeling state of others, or run and hide, you are hooked.
- Don't confuse legitimate helping with getting caught in a triangle. In legitimate helping, a problem is temporary and your efforts provide relief. If the problem persists, more help is required than what you can offer. If the problem persists, your helping effort may actually be preventing change.
- Unhooking yourself from a triangle is not very hard. *Remaining unhooked,* while under pressure from others to change back, is difficult and requires perseverance. Hang in there.

Chapter 6

The Second Step:
Changing Your Role in the Problem

My role in the problem? you say to yourself. *I know I'm not a totally innocent by-stander in this relationship, but frankly our problems are mainly his fault, not mine.*
Uh-huh.

When people are calm, level-headed, and content in their relationships, they usually believe the old clichés about marriages and marital woes:

> *It takes two to tango.*
> *Relationships are a two-way street.*
> *Marriages are a fifty-fifty proposition.*
> *There are no innocent victims.*

But when it comes to understanding why it is that in one's own marriage certain conflicts recur without resolution, people drift to the blaming position. They see less and less how they are contributing to a problem and more and more how their mate is causing all the difficulties. They view themselves as tolerant and their efforts at resolving conflicts as reasonable and well-intended. They view their mates as intolerant and their mate's efforts to resolve marital conflicts as unreasonable and a bit malicious.

That outlook—the one that says that one's spouse is primarily to blame and that he has a "bad attitude"—is one of the most common reasons why some marital problems, once begun, can't get resolved. True, one spouse may not have *started* a problem that has become chronic, but the manner in which both partners have *responded* to the problem is keeping it alive. The truth is that partners dedicated to making a marriage work often shoot themselves in the foot (and then wonder why they can't walk through life together and happy). They act in ways that *appear* reasonable and helpful but that are, in fact, *self-defeating*. How so?

"Foot shooters" have a tendency to:

- Discourage a spouse's desirable behavior and encourage undesirable behavior—even when they are doggedly trying to do just the opposite

- Stubbornly reapply "solutions" that rarely worked while abandoning more effective solutions just when progress is being made

- Look for evidence to support preexisting negative beliefs about one's mate while dismissing evidence of to the contrary
- "Push" their spouse's "buttons," then act indignant when their spouse pushes back

Perhaps most important, foot shooters *dismiss the evidence that they themselves are actually making matters worse.* It takes them a little time to admit the truth to themselves.

Are you a foot shooter? Take the following quiz to find out.

Foot Shooter Quiz

Do you and your mate ever have repetitive, no-win, "Here we go again" arguments?
If you answered *"Yes,"* you are a foot shooter. Believe it. It's that simple.

Foot Shooting No More

It's time to remove the bullets from your gun.

The "bullets" in this case are the beliefs, attitudes, words, and behaviors that have not helped you in your efforts to improve your marriage. If you *think differently* and *act differently* with respect to your mate, the issues that now divide you will either disappear or will no longer make a difference. Don't believe me? Let me say it more convincingly:

If you stopped shooting yourself in the foot, 50 to 75 percent of all your arguments and disagreements would vanish almost immediately! Why? Because it is the mutual hurt feelings that arise from misguided efforts to solve problems that fuel future arguments. When you and your mate *repeatedly* argue about money, for instance, it is no longer spending habits that divide you. You're more hurt and angry over your mate's *style* of problem solving than by his point of view. Now you regard him as insensitive or controlling or demanding or whatever—and it is that perception which keeps your hurt alive.

So by altering your own self-defeating patterns, you dramatically reduce the misunderstandings and hurt feelings, which makes problem solving a fairly easy task.

How to Begin

Essentially, you must alter *just a few* fundamental beliefs and certain patterns of behaving.

As intelligent human beings, we all rely on our perceptions and ideas to guide us safely through the day. So it is unsettling to learn that some of our perceptions are distorted and our ideas mistaken. It may be that we are not wrong in our perceptions; we are simply not seeing all that is there. Magicians make their living by exploiting the human tendency to misperceive. Ever drive on a highway and see what appears to be water shimmering on the road up ahead? Then, as you drive closer, the "water" disappears. What you thought you saw never was. Ever feel extremely self-conscious about a facial blemish, only to have your friend tell you, "I never noticed it until you mentioned it"? Was the blemish obvious to all or wasn't it? The "truth" may not be what you believe. In fact, when it comes to relationships, the "truth" is rarely all that you think it is.

Attitude Shift One

Begin to believe that your spouse says and does hurtful and counterproductive things for one of two reasons: he is afraid and worried, or he actually thinks he's being helpful.

You think he does some things just to be mean? You're right, he probably does. Sometimes. But why does he want to be mean? *Because he's angry.* Why is he angry? *Because he feels mistreated and hurt.* (Bear with me here. I know you may feel he has no right to feel mistreated or hurt, but believe me, he does feel that way.) How was he hurt? *Somehow, in your interactions with him, he experienced a loss of love (he felt rejected or ignored), a loss of self-esteem (he felt criticized), or a loss of influence over important matters in his life (he felt you were too controlling).* Feeling unloved, disrespected, or less competent and in control frightened and worried him. So he responded in a manner that hurt you. It wasn't right that he did that, but you need to know he did it primarily because he was afraid.

Most of the time, hurtful spouses are also trying very hard to be helpful. But because they are exceptional foot shooters, things didn't work out quite like they expected.

Dick often had to bring paperwork home on the weekends, much to Martha's displeasure. Not only did Martha wish she could see more of Dick on the weekends, she wasn't thrilled with having the brunt of all the child care chores while Dick was preoccupied. Dick sensed that about Martha, so he took frequent breaks from his work to play with the kids, fix them their lunch, or do what needed to be done so that Martha could have some free time to herself. In short, he was trying to be helpful.

But Martha saw things differently. She thought Dick would get his work done sooner if he wouldn't take so many breaks. She thought he procrastinated—thereby prolonging his involvement with his work unnecessarily. Moreover, although she often wanted Dick's help with something, she never bothered to ask him while he was working, because she was trying to be helpful. As a result, when she did ask for help, she felt entitled to it. After all, it isn't easy being a single parent on weekends. So she wouldn't "ask" for his help, she'd *insist.* And Dick resented her discourteous and angry tone of voice. After all, he'd helped her numerous times without having to be asked, so he felt entitled to some courtesy from her. Still wanting to be helpful, he'd comply with her request for assistance, but grudgingly. Martha sensed his "attitude" and resented it. *I can't believe this husband of mine,* Martha said to herself. *You'd think he'd be happy to help me out after all I've done for him.* So Martha developed an "attitude" too.

Ironically, Dick's efforts to spend more time with the family and less on paperwork prompted Martha to be *unappreciative*—the very opposite of what was intended. And Martha's efforts not to bother Dick unless it was absolutely necessary prompted Dick to be *unappreciative and resentful*—the very opposite of what was intended.

Martha and Dick are typical. They try to be helpful, shoot themselves in the foot instead, and temporarily cripple the relationship.

If you can believe that once in a while YOU say or do hurtful things because you're worried about how lovable you are or about the state of the marriage, then start believing the same about your spouse.

If you can believe that once in a while YOU say or do wrong things but with the right intentions, then start believing the same about your spouse.

Attitude Shift Two
Begin to believe that sometimes spouses say or do hurtful or insensitive things for understandable reasons that have absolutely nothing to do with the relationship.

We know that our children get cranky when they are hungry, hot, or overtired, but we usually (and unfairly) expect our mate to be "mature" and immune to the emotional impact that hunger, heat, or exhaustion can have. Yet fast-paced life styles, job pressures, demands from children, and poor health habits (overeating, underexercising) do affect our moods and our capacity to deal with daily hassles in a tolerant, level-headed manner.

Gail was unhappy with her extra weight. When her husband Art hugged her, she stiffened and pulled away, feeling unattractive. Of course, being a man, Art took it personally. And since he had just arrived home after being stuck in traffic for thirty minutes in a car with no air conditioning—and since he was starving for dinner—he was in no mood for games.

"Have it your way," he said angrily, walking away from her.

That only reinforced Gail's view that she had lost her sex appeal. They did not have a good night together.

Don't overlook the obvious. Certain times of day are more stressful than others and may explain why your mate seems difficult or uncooperative. Certain situations are also inherently more stressful (such as driving many hours in a car full of kids) and may explain for why your mate is in a foul mood.

Attitude Shift Three

Begin to believe that your interpretations of your spouse's behavior are formed in part by the mood you were in at the time.

I'm sure there were times in your life when you were in such a good mood that events that might ordinarily upset you (a broken plate, a bounced check) didn't have such a negative impact. And I'm sure there were times when you were in such a bad mood that events that ordinarily wouldn't annoy you prompted you to lose your temper ("Aargh! Who put fingerprints all over this refrigerator!"). Obviously our moods affect the way we interpret events and how we respond to those events. But in marriages soured by repetitive arguments, partners lose sight of that simple fact.

If you are worried that your spouse has lost interest in you, then certain "neutral" behaviors will be suspect (such as arriving home later than expected).

If you are angry, then the moment he leaves your side at a party, you'll think he was rude to do so.

If you are feeling guilty for something you said or did (or didn't do), then the moment your mate appears sullen, you'll feel responsible.

The truth is, *we do tend to interpret events in light of our current mood.* Bear that in mind the next time you believe your mate is being unkind, critical, or insensitive.

Attitude Shift Four

Begin to believe that your interpretations of your spouse's current behavior are formed in part by your preexisting beliefs about your mate.

Dissatisfied spouses become expert labelers. They label their mate in some negative way ("She's just being stubborn" or "He's controlling") and pretty soon the label sticks. Then, any time their mate takes a strong view of something, "She's being stubborn again" or "He's trying to have things his way again." (See "Marriage Matters" on the following page.) As I pointed out in chapter 1, frustrated spouses—instead of questioning their own judgment—strongly believe that their negative perceptions are accurate. Consequently, they regard their mate as deserving of punishment, which only adds to the discord.

Once a mate is negatively labeled, evidence is sought to support the view. Evidence to the contrary is overlooked. This bias in perception is not done maliciously. It is done primarily out of fear and a need to protect oneself. For example, if you believed while walking a dark street that someone was following you, you would focus on any evidence to support that belief—an unusual noise, the sound of another's footsteps, etc. And if someone was indeed out to harm you, your awareness of that might give you a protective edge. But what if you were mistaken? Or what if someone was behind you but was not following you? Then you worried for nothing. Unfortunately, many couples have a fixed negative belief about their mate that prompts them to search for supporting evidence. And they may "find" it—just as the person walking found evidence of being followed—but their original premise may be mistaken.

If you have a fixed negative belief about your mate, consider *alternative* explanations for his behavior, explanations that don't make him seem so nasty. After all, whenever you say or do something nasty, aren't you able to explain it to yourself in a way that doesn't make you seem like such a bad person?

MARRIAGE MATTERS

Negative labels do stick, and discontented spouses often don't give their mates credit when it is deserved.

In one study,[1] couples were evaluated to determine their level of marital happiness. The happiest and unhappiest were then asked to discuss an area of conflict. But one person from each marriage was secretly taken aside and told by the researchers to be especially "positive" or "negative" during their discussion with their mate. The purpose of the study was to determine how the unsuspecting spouses would interpret why their mate was so cooperative or so difficult.

The results showed that the rationale spouses gave for their partner's behavior had everything to do with preexisting beliefs and current moods. Spouses unhappy in their marriage had a preexisting negative view. Thus, they attributed their mate's "negative" or uncooperative behavior as due to a character flaw ("He's always disagreeable"). Unhappy spouses attributed their partner's cooperative behavior as due to extenuating circumstances ("He must have had a good day at work").

Happy couples did the opposite. They attributed a partner's positive behavior to character ("He's always like that") and viewed negatively as caused by extenuating circumstances ("He must have had a hectic day at the office").

The study underscores the observation that when couples aren't getting along, anything one does right will still be wrong (or at least unappreciated). And when couples are happy and content, anything one does wrong will be okay (or at least forgiven).

The Behavioral Shift

In chapter 3 you saw that people tend to cope with conflict in one of four unproductive ways: They *fight* (complain, argue, blame, coerce); they *flee* (refuse to talk, spend time away, become addicted to alcohol, drugs, or work); they *freeze* (procrastinate, stay indecisive); or they *fold* (surrender, give in).

If you tend to act in one or more of those ways as a matter of routine when dealing with marital issues, you have helped perpetuate marital distress. Sorry, but it's true. While the *fight* stance most obviously adds to the difficulties, the other three stances, though often used to *prevent or avoid* conflict, paradoxically increase the odds that conflict (or unhappiness) will persist. Partners who *flee* or *withdraw* from conflict or conversation as a way to keep the peace have chosen a particularly counterproductive approach. (This is similar to someone who avoids a dentist out of fear. Because his teeth are not being properly cleaned and checked, tooth or gum problems develop. But now he is even more reluctant to see a dentist because so much repair work will have to be done. Ouch!)

Behavioral Shift One

Identify which of the four unproductive coping styles you tend to use (fight, flee, freeze, or fold) and begin to switch to a healthier problem-solving style.

It is unreasonable to expect you to change one of these patterns quickly or easily. But it can be accomplished, and with less discomfort than you imagine. Your ultimate goal is to cope with conflict by talking (not yelling), understanding (not judging), listening (not tuning out), generating possible solutions (not insisting that your way is the only way), and giving a mutually agreed-upon solution an honest try (not dumping it at the first sign of backsliding).

Phew! Sounds challenging, doesn't it? Actually, it isn't that difficult, but it does require patience and practice. Tips to make it easier:

- When you notice yourself going back to your old, unproductive ways, admit it to your mate. Saying, "I just started judging you. I don't want to do that, so please bear with me" will inform him that you do care about his feelings and want matters to improve.

- If you don't have a clue what to say or do that will improve a bad situation, say that to your spouse. "I'm feeling stuck now. I want us to do this better, but I'm unsure what to do. Can you help me out?" Even if no ideas come to mind, you've probably already helped the situation by those words. Why? Because *your major problem is not the issue that currently divides you.* It is any bad feelings that have developed as a consequence of having mishandled the issue. Informing your mate that you sincerely wish things to be better can soothe some hurt feelings.

- Reach over and touch your mate in a gesture of caring. Placing your hand over hers or touching her shoulder can soften hard feelings at critical moments. If she flinches or pulls back, don't get bent out of shape. Saying, "I want you to know I still care" can help.

- Respond first to what your mate says that has merit or makes sense. Don't automatically respond to what you disagree with. Remember, partners sometimes stubbornly maintain a viewpoint not because they're convinced they are 100 percent correct but because they're annoyed and offended to find their concerns or ideas dismissed so readily.

- When you want to debate your mate or defend your position, you increase the odds that the discussion will get out of hand. You have time to state your point of view, but first *summarize your understanding of what your partner just told you.* "So you're telling me I'm spending too much money on items we don't need. Is that right?" By summarizing, your mate will know you've listened, any misunderstandings can be quickly corrected, and you buy yourself time to think about what you want to say instead of automatically saying what you think.

- End any conversation, however imperfect it was, with a caring gesture. You may not feel understood or appreciated, but patting his back or squeezing his hand will ease any tension and relieve some hurt feelings. You may not feel like touching, but do it anyway. It only takes half a second and can prevent hours of aggravation.

As you may have noticed, none of the above tips tell you how to solve whatever issue divides you. Resolving that issue is less important right now. It bears repeating that *once a conflict has become chronic, the primary focus must be on soothing the bad feelings that have resulted, not on solving the original problem.*

Most people believe that if you can finally solve a recurrent problem, any of the nasty side effects of that problem (the hurt feelings, the mistrust, etc.) will disappear. (It is that common-sense but incorrect assumption that prompts very intelligent people to keep hammering away at the same issue—to no avail.) The truth is that when problems recur, *until you can soothe the bad feelings, the original problem MAY NEVER GET RESOLVED TO YOUR MUTUAL SATISFACTION!**

Behavioral Shift Two
Halt repeated efforts to get your spouse to change.

You have a right and an obligation to talk with your mate about marital concerns. If your mate is hurting you in some way, by all means tell him to stop. But if you've repeatedly invested heaps of emotional energy to get your spouse to be different—if you've complained, badgered, punished, withdrawn in a huff, given him the "silent treatment," sweet-talked, given him funny greeting cards, or in any other way cajoled or manipulated him to change—and it hasn't helped—your efforts have become part of the problem. Don't stop because your mate is incorrigible.

---

* This phenomenon is not limited to marriage conflicts. Consider the Israeli-Arab conflict or the conflict between Catholics and Protestants in Northern Ireland. The points of view that originally divided them have been compounded by year after year of killing and violence. It is no longer a different viewpoint that divides those people—they are angry over continued acts of violence and perceived injustice. No accord they may reach (like the one reached by the Israeli's and the PLO in 1993) will automatically cause their bad feelings to wither.

Stop because your efforts, however reasonable they seemed, were self-defeating. You shot yourself in the foot. Believe me, your mate is being stubborn not because he couldn't care less about your feelings but because he has perceived you to be unreasonable, demanding, insensitive, and hard to satisfy, and he is offended by that. In fact, his stubbornness *is his persistent effort to get YOU to change.* He's hoping that if he acts uncooperatively, you'll back off. But you haven't, have you? *If his persistent efforts to get you to change have failed miserably, why do you think that your persistent efforts to get him to change will succeed?*

Think. What's really bothering you right now is not that he is different from you in ways that are frustrating (maybe he doesn't like to talk much and you do; maybe he's a neatnik and you're not). What's *really* bothering you is your belief that he must not care about your feelings for him to have been so stubborn and difficult. After all, your initial requests for him to change were probably polite and considerate, right? So you've stubbornly attempted to get him to change because you've been hurt by his uncooperative attitude. But *he's* stubbornly tried to get you to change because he's been hurt by your uncooperative attitude. Another fine mess . . .

Should you just stop your efforts and hope matters will improve? No. First, he won't notice right away when you do stop. Second, if you're still angry, he'll interpret your backing off as your way of punishing him. In other words, he'll still think you are trying to get him to change, but he'll think you're trying to achieve that by *pretending* to give up on your quest. Consequently, he won't change. Or if he does make some moves to accommodate you, you won't appreciate it "after all I've had to go through to get him to change . . ."

First, you must really believe that your failed efforts, however well-intentioned, only aggravated the situation. By blaming him less and accepting your role in the continuation of your marital difficulties, you can detach more easily from your efforts to change him.

Second, talk with him (or send him a letter) about how your frustration with him prompted you to act in ways that probably offended him, which caused him to act in ways that offended you, and so on. Tell him there are still some changes you'd like to see but that there are changes he'd probably like to see too. "Can you help me with this? I'm in a dilemma. I want some things to be different but I don't want to convey that somehow you are unacceptable the way you are. Got any ideas?" That approach is less hostile and demanding and may very well help. Consider this: Rarely do partners need to make a 180-degree turn in order to please a mate. In my experience, a fifteen-degree shift by each partner is more than adequate. That's not much, is it?

Lastly, consider this: Sometimes people who are overinvolved in getting their mate to change are underinvolved in some other important aspect of life. Are you underinvolved with your children? with a challenging career or hobby? with attending to your physical health and fitness? with your friends or relatives? If so, involving yourself more in some neglected area may improve your mood and make you less dependent upon your mate for satisfaction.

Behavioral Shift Three

Stop applying "solutions" that have not worked. Chances are you and your mate are locked in a circular pattern whereby the more you do X, the more she does Y, which causes you to do more of X, and so on.

One of the most outstanding behavioral patterns of couples burdened by recurrent conflict is this: Each acts in a way that unwittingly encourages his or her partner to do more of that which is undesirable. For example,

- A wife complains about an issue for the third time because she didn't feel her husband paid attention the first two times. The husband is annoyed that she repeats herself, so he tunes her out, compelling her to complain a fourth time, since once again he is not paying attention.

- A husband expects his wife to protest when he makes a request, so he asks her with sarcasm in his voice. She objects to his tone so denies his request. The next time he uses even more sarcasm.

- A husband who is not often affectionate when making love may prompt his wife to be less available sexually. His need for sex consequently increases, making him more likely to push for "something more" the next time his wife shows affection, thereby reinforcing her belief that "he's only after one thing."

- A wife who believes her mate is avoiding conversation calls him at work "just to chat." He is annoyed that his work time is disturbed for idle chatter. That intensifies her belief that he is avoiding her and prompts her to insist on conversations even at inopportune times. ("I know it's two in the morning but I think we should talk . . .")

- A husband spends more time at work because he is unhappy at home. That adds to his wife's displeasure, which prompts him to want to continue to work overtime.

- A couple bail their twenty-four-year-old son out of one financial mess after another. Knowing he has back-up, the son never takes his spending habits seriously, which eventually causes him to get into debt once again, prompting his parents to bail him out once again.

Such circular patterns are often found in couples who possess opposite traits: assertive/unassertive; spender/miser; optimistic/pessimistic; emotional/logical; pursuer/distancer; spontaneous/planner; introvert/life-of-the-party, etc. The more one partner behaves in one way, the more the other compensates and behaves in another way.

It is no accident that you married someone with opposing traits. Often those opposing traits are *undeveloped qualities within oneself;* for instance, an unassertive man may marry an assertive woman because his assertive qualities are underdeveloped. Sometimes the undeveloped qualities are qualities one wishes to possess but fears. For example, a pessimistic person may wish to be optimistic but fears having his hopes dashed. Or an introvert sees some sense in being extroverted but fears making a fool of himself or being in the spotlight. Spouses with this wish/fear dilemma often criticize their partner for displaying the very qualities they wish they could display.

Halting the circular pattern of responding can be aided by doing two things:

1. Define what it is you are doing that may be causing you and your mate to go in circles, and define why you are doing it. For example:

   "I mumble when my mate talks to me [defining *what* you do] so she'll get the message I don't want to talk" [defining *why* you do it].

   "I criticize my husband when he gets bored while shopping with me [defining *what* you do] so that he'll learn to be more enthusiastic" [defining *why* you do it].

   "I wait for my wife to tell me what she needs from me [defining *what* you do] because I'm afraid to say or do the wrong thing" [defining *why* you do it].

   Now, repeat aloud five times exactly what you've been doing and why you do it.

   Ask yourself: Has it helped? If the answer is *"No,"* stop doing it.

2. Consider the possibility that the qualities you object to in your mate are qualities you've underdeveloped in yourself. Or consider that you may have come to *rely* on your partner's qualities to balance you out. Let's face it, a logical, unemotional spouse can be a source of strength when calmness and clear thinking are required. A spouse who spends money "unnecessarily" has probably purchased things you now enjoy using.

Behavioral Shift Four
Don't abandon solutions (that show promise) at the first sign of difficulty.

You may believe that once changes have begun in a desired direction you'll be thrilled, or at least satisfied. Don't be surprised if you're not. In fact, one way that foot shooters respond to changes is to get "fed up" or impatient *precisely when some progress is underway.* How can that be? One reason is that they *doubt any progress will be permanent,* so they bail out before they get their hopes too high.

Another is that once desired changes are *finally* underway, they get angry that it has taken their spouse so long to be cooperative. Their anger has the effect of stalling any further progress.

Another reason people abandon helpful solutions too early is their false belief that changes should be made without much fuss, fanfare, or backsliding. They don't realize that *backsliding is inevitable* and not merely a sign of lack of trying. So when backsliding occurs, they presume the "solution" was inappropriate and go back to the drawing board. This usually means reverting to old ways of responding (fighting, fleeing, freezing, or submitting) *which never helped and always made matters worse.* (Think of someone trying to lose weight. *Successful* dieters often report that in any given week they may *regain* some lost weight, but that over a longer time frame they did lose the weight they wanted. Backsliding is common.)

Your best bet is to understand that change occurs in fits and starts, with occasional backsliding. Also, give any proposed solution an honest try (thirty days is not unreasonable) before you abandon it.

♥ ♥ ♥

BUILDING A SUCCESSFUL RELATIONSHIP

The "Let's Put It behind Us/No, I Want to Talk about It Now" Syndrome

This is one of the more common tug of wars for couples with recurrent conflicts. Typically, the husband wants to let bygones be bygones and believes he's demonstrating maturity and wisdom by not rewashing old laundry. "Hey, you can't change the past. Am I right or am I right?"

Typically, the wife believes matters are being shoved under the rug. She has never sensed that her hurts and concerns have been taken seriously enough by her husband, so she insists on bringing up the past. "Hey, we have to keep talking about our problem because obviously we haven't resolved it. Am I right or what?"

This problem is self-sustaining. The more he wants to forget the past, the more she wants to review it, and vice versa. Insisting you do things your way won't work because he'll resent it. Giving in and doing it your partner's way won't work because eventually you'll resent it.

The solution is to *understand* the concerns each of you has for wanting to do it your way, and then try to address both of your concerns. For example, people who want to put the past behind them are often *concerned* or *afraid* that talking about old wounds will cause an argument. They don't have faith that the topic can be discussed calmly. (Typically such persons *flee* or *withdraw* as a way to deal with conflict.) People who want to bring up past issues do so because those old issues symbolize current concerns that haven't been taken seriously. They use old situations to buttress whatever point they want their mate to understand. (Typically they *fight* as a way to deal with conflict.) Therefore, if they each agree to discuss concerns without provoking an argument, and if they each act in a manner that demonstrates they are taking each other's concerns seriously, bringing up the past or leaving it behind won't be an issue.

♥ ♥ ♥

Keep in Mind

- If you and your mate go around in circles with some problems, YOU have acted in ways that make sense but are actually self-defeating.

- Because some "solutions" to problems make sense ("We need to talk more" or "You need to find a hobby"), they are not abandoned when they've repeatedly failed.

- Often, spouses say or do hurtful or insensitive things out of *fear* or in a misguided effort to be helpful.

- Spouses often dig in their heels and take a stubborn position on some issue not because they believe they are 100 percent correct but because they are offended to find their ideas or concerns dismissed so readily. (But *that* never gets discussed.)

- If you are overinvolved in trying to get your mate to change, you are probably underinvolved in some other important area of your life. Reinvolve yourself in some neglected area and you may discover that your need for your spouse to change has lessened a bit.

Chapter 7

The Third Step:
Uncovering Hidden Agendas

Once you've cleared away the clutter in your relationship problems by dismantling the emotional triangles, and once you focus on *your role* in the maintenance of any recurrent problem (rather than blaming and seeing yourself as a victim), you can dramatically slow the cycle of recurrent conflict.

But more is required.

When the same argument crops up over and over again, you can bet that you and your mate haven't discussed the heart of the matter. Instead, you've argued or debated issues that *symbolize* a deeper, hidden concern. In other words, *your arguments are not what you have been arguing about!*

Matt had been on the phone for over half an hour when Kelly pointed to her watch and said sternly, "How long are you planning to be?" Kelly was annoyed because she and Matt had planned to take a stroll and it was growing dark outside.

Matt put his hand up in a gesture of dismissal. So Kelly left and went for a walk by herself. Matt was off the phone in ten minutes and was angry to discover that Kelly had gone ahead without him.

They argued about it later. Matt was mostly upset by Kelly's "rude way of trying to get me off the phone." He felt embarrassed that his wife had complained to him loudly enough for the person he'd been speaking with to overhear.

"I was not rude," Kelly responded. "You knew we planned to go for a walk but instead you spent all that time on the phone. You could have called back."

"Wait a minute," Matt argued. "We never set a specific time to go walking. It was something we were going to do when we had the time. Besides, I was talking with my brother. How often do I get to do that?"

"Who's more important, your brother or me?" Kelly shot back.

Let's examine their conversation more closely. On the surface they had an annoying but simple misunderstanding. She expected them to go for a walk at a specific time; he had no special time in mind. Their signals got crossed. What's the big deal? It became a big deal when Matt viewed Kelly as being "rude" and Kelly felt dismissed. Then the issue was no longer a misunderstanding; it became *personal.*

The first clue that it was personal was Matt's use of the word "rude." It was an accusatory word, a bit strong and inflammatory. Use of such words in a conversation ("You *nag* . . . you *whine* . . . You're *irresponsible* . . . You *always* do that . . . You *never* do this . . ." etc.) usually signal the presence of a deeper level of frustration, hurt, or anger. **Kelly's comment, *"Who's more important, your brother or me?"* was the next indication that the argument was really about deeper issues.**

Matt and Kelly could continue their argument in a number of ways. For example, they might *debate* whether they had actually preagreed on a specific time to go for a walk, or whether Kelly really had behaved rudely. In other words, they could argue intellectually about the *content*—the "facts" of what happened. This debate will have no satisfying conclusion. Eventually they'll "drop it," but their anger won't truly go away.

Or, since each felt hurt and offended by the other, they could label one another "inconsiderate" or "selfish" and argue about that. In other words, they may stop debating what specifically happened or didn't happen (content) and instead debate the *process* (the *way* each one acted or their *styles* of behavior). They don't like each other's "attitude." That argument, while probably no more helpful than arguing about content, is closer to their hidden, underlying concerns. Kelly is primarily concerned that Matt no longer sees her as a priority in his life. Matt is concerned that Kelly is showing discourtesy and disrespect and therefore may not care about him as she once did.

What is the best way for them to "argue"? The best way would be to use the events that led to their conflict (his being on the telephone, etc.) as a springboard for a discussion about their *broader* worries. Then they may discover that Matt cares about Kelly's concern that she is not important in his life, and that Kelly cares about Matt's concern that she is falling out of love with him. If all they do is accuse and get defensive ("I *do* care about you!"/"No, you *don't!*"), their discussion will go nowhere fast. Again, commenting on what your partner says *that makes some sense* is better than commenting only on what you disagree with. Kelly may adamantly believe she was not rude when she asked Matt how long he'd be on the phone, but Matt will probably be more cooperative if she says, "I didn't intend to be rude, but I can see how you might be bothered by what I did." And Matt may adamantly believe that they had not agreed on a specific time to go for a walk, but Kelly might feel better if he says, "I really didn't think I was keeping you waiting, but I can understand why you might think I was."

If Matt and Kelly never get to that third way of discussing their concerns, their argument will recycle. It may be an argument about some other issue entirely (not having cleaned out her car after he promised he would), but deep down it will be about the same fundamental concerns that prompted their previous argument.

Clues to Hidden Agendas

Because hidden agendas are, by definition, concealed or disguised, couples may not recognize that they are lurking. One clue to hidden agendas is recurrent, if-it's-not-one-thing-it's-another, conflict. Another clue is the use of provocative or inflammatory language.

Still other clues are:

- Flash-fire displays of anger that seemingly comes from nowhere
- Anger about "little things"
- Anxiety about raising certain topics
- Asking "why" questions when no answer would be good enough ("Why do you spend more time at work than with your family?")
- "Solutions" that never seem to work
- "Agreements" that never get acted on
- Feeling lonely or ill at ease with your mate
- Thinking that the relationship is somehow "unfair"
- Communication patterns punctuated by hinting, innuendos, or ambiguous physical gestures instead of straightforward discussions

The presence of some of these clues does not automatically mean a relationship issue is hidden. Sometimes people have big flare-ups over little things because they're just having a bad day. But if any of the clues persist, chances are some relationship issues are not being addressed.

"I Understand What You're Saying, BUT . . ."

Be careful. Since couples know they are supposed to show understanding to a disgruntled mate, they often spout the words "I understand, but . . ." But what? The "but" in your viewpoint, however logical, probably won't excite your mate. Saying "but" shows a greater concern for being understood (or agreed with) than for understanding.

Couples who fight about everything except what's *really* bothering them essentially *do not feel understood* by their mate. A good rule to follow any time you and your mate are bickering or doing a "slow burn" is to tell your mate, "There is probably something you want me to understand right now that you don't think I do understand. Please tell me and I promise to listen." Once your mate has spoken, *summarize* what he just said before you give your point of view.

But even if a spouse does feel understood, it may not be enough. Spouses must also feel *cared about* by their mate. They must believe their concerns are *taken seriously* and not dismissed as childish or unimportant. They must believe they are *acceptable* even though they are not perfect. The problem is that it is difficult to listen, accept, and take your partner seriously when you honestly don't think your mate is giving you the same courtesy. But someone has to start. (I know. You did start, many times. And it hasn't "worked." However, my guess is that your spouse believes he tried to be the magnanimous one many times and his efforts didn't work either. Remember, far from not trying hard enough, most spouses believe they have done more than their share to improve a troubled relationship. Try again. This time, keep it up for at least several weeks and let your mate know what you are doing and why.)

Too often, couples in conflict not only disagree about "what" happened, they accuse their mates of being wrong for *feeling* a certain way. Simply put, *whenever you tell your mate that he or she shouldn't feel the way he or she feels, you do not understand.* Your partner's feelings *do make sense* once you understand his or her perspective.

Failure to communicate understanding or acceptance will make simple discussions complicated or even destructive. The ability to communicate understanding and acceptance can make potentially difficult discussions simple and satisfying.

Different Kinds of Hidden Agendas

Esteemed marital researcher Dr. John Gottman at the University of Washington has thoroughly analyzed how couples deal with conflict. When a couple is discussing a divisive issue, certain signs are highly predictable of future marital distress, even when the couple seem to be getting along at the time they are being studied. Two of the main indicators are:

1. **Withdrawal:** When at least one partner routinely withdraws from conflict or otherwise "shuts down," marital satisfaction deteriorates over time. As I showed in chapter 3, withdrawal can take many forms, including silence, leaving the room, or involving oneself in activities to distract from the issues at hand.

    A spouse who routinely withdraws from conflict or conversation has underlying AGENDAS that are not being addressed.

2. **Defensiveness:** People get defensive when they feel they are being attacked. Accusations and criticism bring on defensiveness almost as surely as night follows day. People in a defensive mode are less interested in working things out than they are protecting themselves. Consequently, defensiveness impedes constructive problem solving.

    When a defensive posture is the rule rather than the exception, hidden agendas are lurking, since issues could not get properly resolved.

Ferreting out the hidden agendas is essential if marital happiness is to improve. In fact, successful couples are adept at unearthing any hidden agendas quickly.

While it may seem that hidden agendas could be varied and numerous, Dr. Gottman's research suggests that all fall into one of only three categories:

- *Am I loved? Cared about? Trusted? Appreciated?* This dimension deals with how positively one believes his or her mate feels toward him or her. A wife who constantly pursues her husband for attention or affection eventually believes he must not care about her.

- *Is my mate interested in me? Attracted to me? Does my mate respond to my needs?* This dimension is concerned with a spouse's *responsiveness* to a partner. Being responsive to a spouse is quite different than saying nice words such as "I love you." According to Dr. Gottman, it is much harder work. It is much action-oriented. "I know he loves me," said one frustrated wife. "I just wish he'd *show* me he loves me."

- *Am I on equal footing in this relationship? Am I being treated fairly?* This dimension concerns *status* and issues of control. A spouse who feels inferior or dominated by his mate may do battle over a number of issues as a way to assert some power.

Hidden agendas may not be hidden to the person who holds them. Spouses may be all too aware of painful concerns about not being loved, responded to, or treated fairly in their relationship. The concerns are often kept hidden, however, because there is uneasiness about expressing them straightforwardly. Unfortunately, when serious concerns are kept under wraps, conversations about "What's the problem?" may be fruitless at best, and possibly detrimental.

You met Tom and Carol in chapter 2. Agreeing never to have children, Carol stunned Tom one day by informing him she changed her mind. She wanted to be a mother. Angry, and scared he might lose Carol, Tom eventually agreed the couple could have a baby "someday" but certainly not now. But Carol was adamant.

"How can you even think about getting pregnant with the economy the way it is?" Tom challenged.

"But I've figured out our projected expenses, Tom. If I don't take maternity leave from work, we'll be able to afford a child."

"You say that now, but what if you change your mind later? And even if you didn't change your mind, we're barely paying our mortgage as it is. Do you know how much diapers alone can cost?"

Their arguments went around and around without resolution. Carol always had a plan for saving money and Tom always had a fix on the hidden expenses that can burden any couple trying to make ends meet.

They discussed the topic as if it were a logical matter and devoted energy to persuading one another to "see things my way." But logic had little to do with their impasse. Each had a hidden agenda that was not being addressed but that propelled each of them to take a stubborn position in their standoff. In their case, their agenda was identical and it had to do with status. Carol felt that Tom gave himself final say over major decisions, and she resented it. It was he who decided they would buy a home. It was he who decided the kind of car they would drive. Always Tom, never her.

Ironically, Tom believed that *Carol* was the controlling one. *She* decided how to decorate their rooms. *She* always managed to have them go to her parent's house on Christmas and Thanksgiving each year. (They always visited his parents the night before or the day after.) *She* decided when they'd socialize. And when it came to sex, well, she said "No" a lot more often than he ever did.

Clearly they've been jockeying for the leader position for quite some time without ever having sat down and discussed it. Until they address their underlying concerns about unfairness, their resentment and dissatisfaction will fester—whether or not Carol ever gets pregnant.

A useful conversation between them might begin like this:

"Carol, the more I think about it the more I realize that it isn't just child expenses that worry me. For a long time I've felt that when it comes to certain issues—like whose parents to visit on Christmas, or even what kind of laundry detergent to buy—you insist on doing things your way. I feel like my opinion doesn't matter and my feelings don't count."

Now Tom has certainly said a mouthful here. Even if Carol is in the best of moods she could still get defensive, telling Tom she's dumbfounded that he would think *she* has all the decision-making power. How could he be so blind? Although tempted to say that, she nonetheless chooses first to *summarize* what she has heard.

"So you're telling me that I don't consider what you might want, and I make sure we do things my way?"

Tom is surprised by her lack of defensiveness.

"Well, it isn't all the time," he answers. "But much of the time I feel that way."

Before Carol tells him her side of the story, she does one more smart thing. She *empathizes* with him.

"That must be an awful way to feel," she says.

By this time, Tom feels listened to and understood. He also feels that she cares about his feelings. Consequently, he is ready to hear her viewpoint without much criticism.

"I know it's an awful way to feel, Tom, because I've been feeling the same way. I remember when we bought the house, you decided when and where and how much. And you know the truck you bought? I wanted a car. But I went along with your decision—not that I liked it."

In an ideal conversation, Tom and Carol might begin to discover that they have often unwittingly *reinforced* in each other the "we're going to do it my way" stance.

The more Tom has believed Carol to be controlling and dictatorial, the more he has put his foot down on some issues. But the more "inflexible" he became, the more likely she has been to insist on doing things her way. As they discuss the matter further, Tom admits that Carol's budget ideas are sound and that they can probably afford a baby. He has never admitted that before, because, despite her sound reasoning about their finances, he has felt that her persuasive efforts were nothing more than an attempt to get her own way without concern for him. Indeed, acknowledging that they can afford a baby doesn't solve their problem, since affordability was never the real issue. So each agrees to speak up immediately when they feel controlled or dominated by the other. Then they will discuss the matter in a way that shows concern for the other's feelings and viewpoint. The more they succeed in doing that, the less they will compete for the job of CEO in their marriage.

As you can see, without a (constructive and respectful) discussion about their hidden agendas, they might have fought about their budget for months to no avail.

♥ ♥ ♥

MARRIAGE MATTERS

How important is equality in a marriage? Very. In a study reported in the *Journal of Family Psychology*[1], researcher Erich Kirchler showed that happy couples experienced an *equal balance of power* in the relationship that places them in contrast to moderately unhappy couples.

In unequal relationships, the more unequal the *overt* power, the more the one-down spouse may try to gain power *covertly*. By strategic use of procrastination, hedging, or subtle acts of "sticking it" to their mate, the one-down partner can easily complicate the dominant partner's life.

The research study also revealed that marital happiness was a by-product of the couple's ability to perceive each other's emotional state and needs accurately. Moderately unhappy couples were not adept at this. But even happy couples were less adept when conflict was high. The anxiety that conflict brings on seems to interfere with a spouse's capacity to perceive his or her partner's emotional needs adequately. Power struggles can be a constant undercurrent of tension in a marriage and lead to distortion of perceptions. Distorted perceptions about one's mate can lead to unfair attacks or manipulations to gain control—which will lead to more power struggles, more tension, and more misperceptions.

♥ ♥ ♥

Tim was underneath his car attempting to repair it. Tools were scattered over the driveway. He heard Amy's call, insisting he come in the house and watch the children while she went on an errand. *"Oh for God's sake,"* he mumbled to himself.

Once inside the house, Tim was dismayed to find that Amy was far from ready to leave. After waiting ten minutes, he stormed outside and resumed worked on his car.

Amy was not amused.

Let's rewind this tape and view it from Amy's perspective. She'd been watching the clock for the past hour. Tim had promised to be ready by two o'clock so she could do some shopping. He had had all morning to work on the car. She understood that the car needed fixing, but resented that Tim always found some chore to do on a Saturday that kept him away from her and the kids. By three o'clock she was fuming. *Doesn't he care about what's important to me?* she mumbled to herself. So she yelled at him to come inside. As he did so, she changed the baby's diaper (Tim's hands were too greasy to do it), and then wiped up red juice that had exploded from their four-year-old's juice box ("I just squeezed it a little bit, Mom.") A quick brush of her hair, locate her shoes, and she'd be ready. In the meantime, Tim stalked about in the kitchen like an impatient tiger. Finally ready to leave, she looked around. No Tim. *If he went back outside, I'll . . .*

Like most arguments where hidden agendas are not revealed, Tim and Amy then threw "facts" at each other without addressing the more fundamental issues:

> HER FACT: "You said you'd be finished fixing the car by two o'clock. I waited until three before I asked you to come in."
>
> HIS FACT: "I lost track of the time. All you had to do was come and get me at two o'clock. And when you did call me, you didn't 'ask' me to come inside. You demanded it."
>
> HER FACT: "I'm already late, I'm scurrying around trying to clean up spilled juice and change the baby's diaper—and YOU go back outside!"
>
> HIS FACT: "Well YOU weren't ready to leave! I had more work to do!"

When they ran out of facts for the current problem, they threw in facts of previous unresolved problems:

> HER FACT: "Why is it you can find time for all the fix-it chores you have but you don't find time for me when I want it?"
>
> HIS FACT: "We just spent an entire weekend together last weekend. Have you forgotten that already? And those chores I do that you complain about are necessary. Do you think I enjoy spending eight hours on a Saturday underneath a filthy engine?"

At that point their hidden agendas were raised, although not in a constructive fashion. She was feeling he took little interest in her anymore. She wondered whether he was still attracted to her. They rarely talked the way they used to. What was wrong? And he felt thoroughly unappreciated for all his efforts. He worked hard all week, repaired household items on weekends, never complained when she needed his help with something ("Tell me what to do and I'll do it" is his code). And in return he hears complaints, sighs, demands, and no goddamn appreciation. *Does she really care about me?* he wonders. *Maybe I'll finally get the appreciation I deserve after suffering a heart attack, if I survive it . . .*

If they fail to address the hidden agenda, you can bet that one day next week he'll come home exhausted from work and want only to sit in his favorite chair and watch the news. She'll see that as more evidence of being ignored by him, and she'll comment on it. He'll view her complaint as more evidence of being unappreciated, sigh loudly, and roll his eyes. If he's too tired to argue, he'll dutifully turn off the television and announce his availability to her for the rest of the evening.

"Just tell me what to do . . ."

"And you'll do it. I know, I know. That's all you ever say, Tim."

"Well? What else do you want me to say, Amy?"

"Forget it. Just watch television and forget it."

There is still much hope for Tim and Amy, if they follow these guidelines for addressing hidden agendas:

1. Once you notice that a discussion/argument is getting nowhere, call a TIME-OUT.

2. Determine whether what's really bothering you has to do with one of the three hidden agenda dimensions (not feeling loved or cared about, not feeling your mate is interested in you, not feeling equal in the relationship).

3. If you locate a hidden agenda, tell your mate. Don't discuss the current argument any further except to help explain your hidden agenda.

4. Ask whether your mate has a hidden agenda. Make it matter to you to hear what that might be.

5. Once you've identified the *real* problem, talk about what each of you can start doing differently that would help. Be precise. Make a short list of things you are willing to do right away, and start doing them.

6. Touch base with each other within a week to assess how the changes are working. Make corrections as needed.

It is also a good idea to mention to your mate any time your hidden agenda issue gets provoked during the week. Don't accuse. Inform. It's a bit troublesome to do this at first, but it gets easier.

BUILDING A SUCCESSFUL RELATIONSHIP

According to author Richard Driscoll,[2] spouses sometimes regard the words "I understand" as meaning "I agree with you" or "I will support you." Misinterpretations of language can send a couple already dissatisfied with one another into fits of frustration and despair.

Imagine that a husband "understands" the emotional angst his wife is experiencing in her troubled relationship with her parents. But the next time her parents are visiting, she gets angry that her husband didn't "support me" when an argument with her parents flared. In this case, she confused "understanding" with getting support. The two have different meanings. If the problem is that you want a mate to be more supportive, better to say that than to accuse him or her of not understanding. "I'm aware that you understand what I'm feeling," you might say, "but I need you to be more supportive of what I'm going through."

Remember, a spouse may understand you but disagree with you. A spouse may disagree with you but be willing to support you on some issue. A spouse may understand and agree with you, but be unwilling to support you on some issue.

♥ ♥ ♥

Keep in Mind

- When arguments recycle, you are no longer arguing about what you thought you were arguing about.

- Debating the "facts" of what happened is unproductive after the first airing.

- Don't be shocked and dismayed that your partner views events from a different perspective. Your goal is to understand one another's perspective, not belittle it.

- Any time you tell your mate "You shouldn't feel that way," you do not understand him and he's lonelier for it.

- Don't turn revelations of hidden agendas into accusations. They are explanations of feelings.

Chapter 8

The Fourth Step: Shedding Light on Your Past

Rotten luck. That's what Laura believes about her choice of Will as a mate. She's bubbly, full of life, and as emotional as Niagara Falls is wet. What could she have seen in Will? Granted, he is a nice guy. But he's so *boring.* Give him quiet music and the Sunday newspaper and you won't hear from him for days. Still, they've managed to stay married for fourteen years. Laura doesn't quite know why, given all their arguments and stalemates through the years.

Will shakes his head with a puzzled, "I can't figure her out" look. "Essentially, she's hard to satisfy. Last year when we drove through Nebraska we went by acres of wheat fields. She was bowled over by their vastness. She wanted to know my reaction. I said the fields were pretty. *'Pretty?'* she said. 'Is that all you can say?' How much can a person say about a wheat field? It's times like that when I wonder how we've stayed married so long."

Will and Laura are not uncommon. Many spouses have opposite qualities that can drive one another batty at times. But it is a mistake to think that a partner's faults have nothing whatsoever to do with our own psychological make-up. Except for rare exceptions, it is no accident that you married who you married.

Have You Come to Terms with Your Past?

Couples with recurrent conflicts can often get to the heart of the matter without emphasizing their childhood experiences. Many arguments and misunderstandings can be cleared up with mixture of open-mindedness, level-headedness, kindness, and honesty. Even if a childhood issue is the reason a problem began (say, a husband is overly suspicious that his wife is having an affair because his mother had affairs), that issue is often not the reason why the problem persists. (His constant mistrust of her corrodes her affection for him, prompting her to fantasize about other men.) The first seven chapters in this book have shown that spouses frequently respond to marital problems in self-defeating ways, thereby prolonging or worsening the very problems they hoped to eradicate.

Still, if the same conflicts reappear in a marriage, and if negative attitudes harden, it is likely that one's past has something to do with present, ongoing problems. Just how much it has to do with current problems isn't always clear.

How you were treated in the past doesn't necessarily predict how you will behave today. For example, a person whose parents were loud and critical may grow up to be loud and critical or softspoken and nonjudgmental.

A child raised by a very permissive parent may adopt few standards as an adult *or* adopt rigid standards.

Authoritative parents may raise children who blindly obey *or* who rebel.

Highly conflictual parents may raise children who fight and argue *or* who avoid fighting.

An adult whose family moved many times when he was a boy may feel edgy when he has lived in one place too long *or* he may yearn to remain in one place.

John and Cindy were raised by a highly anxious mother. John now suffers bouts of panic, while Cindy is the calm, reassuring one in the family.

Jenny's Dad was tight with money. Jenny spends money freely, much to the chagrin of her penny-pinching husband, Al. Al's Dad brought his family to bankruptcy with his gambling debts.

Many abused children grow up to be abusers. But many also grow up to be champions of their children's rights.

Tight-knit families may produce offspring who later crave togetherness *or* crave aloneness.

A son who grew up with an absent father may be devoted to his own children *or* emotionally distant from them.

The list could go on and on. The point is this: *Most people grow up with a desire to be like their parents in some ways and unlike their parents in other ways.* Usually they wish to adopt those qualities they viewed as positive and healthy and disown those qualities viewed as negative or unhealthy. While that all sounds well and good, it can get complicated when dealing with extreme behaviors. For example, Earl regarded his father as a passive wimp of a man. He watched his mother berate his father continually. Earl grew up and became a rather belligerent, angry, "I won't take nothin' from nobody" person—especially toward his wife. Earl's son lived with his father's anger and grew up to be a softspoken man—somewhat like his *grandfather*. What goes around comes around.

To further complicate matters, many people are *ambivalent* about the ways of their parents. That is, as much as they know intellectually that they do not wish to act like their parents in certain ways, it seems a bit disloyal to want that. Or they marry someone who treats them in ways reminiscent of the way their parents treated them. A woman raised by a verbally abusive father vows never to yell at her children—but she marries a man who apparently has no patience for children's antics. What is that about? Basically it is a game of "This time it will work out the way I want it," with adults replaying scenes from their childhood in the hope that this time it will work out favorably. In essence, it is an *unconscious maneuver* to heal the past. But it always makes marriages more complicated, because in such a case a spouse is no longer viewed as a spouse. He or she is a spouse plus a parent-image. Consequently, spouses are never viewed objectively and realistically.

Sorting through the Past

Much of what psychotherapy has been involved with in the last hundred years has been the impact of the past on one's current life. No one chapter in any book could adequately address that topic. However, there are some essential points about one's past experiences that can propel couples back on track to a more satisfying marriage.

Two primary questions you need to ask yourself:

1. *What was my role in my family growing up?*

    Were you a peacemaker, a troublemaker, a whistleblower? irresponsible or over-responsible? invisible? neglected? scapegoated? Your role served a function in your family. Maybe it helped preserve the peace or the status quo. Maybe you were the joy of a parent whose life would otherwise have been meaningless. Maybe you played out a parent's dream, or fought a parent's battles. The longer you were in the role and the more important that role was to you, the harder it will be to abandon that role even when you outgrow your family and marry.

2. *What did I want from my childhood but never fully obtained?*

    What needs didn't get met? Did you wish to be nurtured more? Did you wish for greater independence? Did you need recognition? More self-confidence? More understanding? Did you need to be treated fairly? Loved? If you didn't get some needs met then, how are you getting them met now?

You are more likely to complicate your marriage when your childhood experiences tended toward the extreme. Children who grew up in homes with *too much* or *too little* of some important ingredient run the risk of being too distant or too needy. Pampered, dependent children may marry someone who can take care of them. Unloved children crave love but may shy away and fear intimacy, since such closeness could never be trusted.

You will probably recreate the role you played in childhood in your adult life— especially in your marriage. If you were a responsible child who took care of others, that role will come easily to you as an adult. If you marry someone accustomed to being taken care of, your roles dovetail nicely. But what if you had mixed feelings about your role? Maybe you were so responsible as a child you missed out on the fun of being a child. Then you may go through a period of resenting the caretaking you must do as an adult. Unfortunately, by that time you may be married with three kids, a dog, and two cats, and spend all your free time coaching Little League. Your spouse is no longer a source of support but a source of weariness and dissatisfaction.

If your role in childhood allowed you no flexibility, then certain childhood needs were inevitably not met. Peacekeepers in families never have the luxury of losing control of *their* feelings. Scapegoats are rarely given credit for what they do right. Whistleblowers were shamed when they told some awful truth. If you were always pampered, you may never have been given room to take charge. If you were busy caring for others, they rarely gave back since you always seemed so mature. *But if you perpetuate your role throughout adulthood, your unmet needs will remain unmet.* And you will probably blame your spouse for it.

Can you make changes now? Certainly, but how well your family of origin made changes can be a factor in determining the ease with which you can change. The more rigid and inflexible and frightened of change your family was, the more difficulty you may have setting things right.

Types of Families/Types of Roles

Getting families to work right often comes down to finding the right mix of intimacy, love, and togetherness. Too much intimacy and togetherness can stifle individual growth. Too little love and closeness can also cause harm. Finding the right balance between togetherness and separateness is a key component in any healthy family.

Dysfunctional families offer too much or too little intimacy.

Families with too much closeness may appear to others to be ideal. That is because one rule of overly close families is never to air dirty laundry in public. Loyalty to family is prized. Individuality can be viewed as disloyalty; consequently, members of such families are used to being controlled, manipulated, or dominated. In extreme cases, family members sacrifice their needs and individuality for the sake of the rest of the family. How?

According to family therapist Gus Napier in his book *The Fragile Bond*, children held tightly by their parents tend to fall into one of three roles.

Dependent children are treated as being younger than they are. They are overprotected, maybe pampered, but not allowed to truly grow up. They develop the attitude of *I can't live without you.* They learn to be weak, needy, and helpless. They may be taught that the world is a frightening place. Often, such children grow up to be warm and friendly adults. But they worry about offending others for fear of being abandoned and having to fend for themselves.

Dependent children are not self-assured. If they are self-reliant they always question their capabilities and may allow others to take over for them even when they can handle matters fine on their own.

If the parent of a dependent child is a martyr type, one who sacrifices over and over for the well-being of the family, the child may feel guilty when behaving independently. The child feels indebted to the parent and reluctant to be emotionally independent from that parent.

Stereotypically, mothers will be inclined to overprotect their children while fathers allow their children to take risks. A woman who herself needs nurturing may overnurture her children. But she may also undernurture them if she resents their neediness and constant demands for attention. A man who needs nurturing may deny that in himself and be less inclined to nurture his children—but chances are he married someone who was willing to nurture enough for both of them.

The Marital Companion Child is a child who somehow got promoted to a level on a par with the parents. In a single-parent family this child may replace the absent spouse as a companion and friend to the remaining spouse. More commonly the role is a fairly benign one, such as when a man and his son are "buddies" or a mother and daughter are "good friends." It becomes a problem when the child is not able to return to the role of child. In the worst case the child is literally the sexual outlet for a parent. In less severe but still somewhat problematic cases, the parent leans on the child for emotional support—usually when the child should be leaning on the parent. Consequently, the children often feel they've "missed out" on experiences they deserved.

While children are growing up, parents can certainly be friendly but cannot be their child's friend. A friend is a peer. Parents are the authority. A mother who is best friends with her teen-age daughter may have difficulty asserting her role as authority figure. Mothers can set curfews; "friends" do not.

Companionate children can feel drained from always having to meet a parent's needs. Thus they may be sensitive to relationships where they always have to give. Often they over-give to their mates a bit grudgingly, wondering when it will be "my turn" but reluctant to take a firm stand.

Parental Children are drawn into responsibilities at a young age. Essentially they miss out on many childhood years because they are kept so busy working, cooking, or taking care of others in the family. In severe cases where one parent is quite dysfunctional (alcoholic, seriously depressed, etc.), the parentified child may actually play the role of parent to his or her own parent. Such children feel very responsible when problems or conflicts emerge in the family. They believe they failed to prevent the conflicts and they believe they are responsible for ending the conflicts. Unlike the dependent child, who has the attitude of *I can't live without you*, the parentified child believes *You can't live without me.* Strong, smart, and dependable, these children come across as not requiring help from others. Deep down, however, they are in desperate need of nurturing and affection, although they are afraid to reveal that about themselves. Indeed, they may be unaware of their own needs for dependency, aware only of other's needs. Such people often describe themselves as able to solve other people's problems but not their own.

As adults, people like this are usually attracted to those who are open about their feelings and needs. They prefer needy people they can care for, although eventually they grow weary and lonely and resentful that they give but never receive.

Whether you were a dependent, companionate, or parental child, it is precisely when you feel dissatisfied with that role in adult life that you can start to change it. Instead of seeking change, however, it is common for people to fall into the trap of blaming their spouse for their current condition rather than seeing how they perpetuated a familiar role. Blaming can keep you stuck. Until you succeed in accepting responsibility for your behavior, you will expect your spouse to change, not you. Or you may leave your spouse but repeat the same problems with a new partner.* Or, your spouse may resist your efforts to change. After all, just as you replayed an old role, so has your spouse. He may be not ready to give up his role just yet. In that case, each of you must be open, honest, nonjudgmental, and willing to commit to the relationship during the sorting-it-out period.

Some families are not close at all. Its members are *disengaged* from one another. In close families, members learn to look to the family to get many needs met. In disengaged families, members learn to look outside the family to get needs met. Disengaged families rarely spend time together in family activities. Fighting is common. Expressing tender feelings is uncommon. Children who grow up in such families learn to fend for themselves and not to trust easily. They are unlikely to wear their feelings on their sleeves. Why take the risk of getting their wrists slapped? They develop an attitude of *I can live without you* or *I don't need anybody.* They are frightened of closeness but unconsciously desirous of it. If they do marry, although they may keep to themselves emotionally, they may nonetheless expect loyalty from their mate and be unable to cope well with signs of disloyalty.

Sibling Position

Nick and Gina were frequently at odds. Each could be "pig-headed" and dictatorial, refusing to budge on some issues when a compromise was possible. One reason they fought had nothing to do with the issues they fought about. It had a lot to do with the fact that each was the first-born in a large family. The oldest child in any family is accustomed to taking on responsibilities and being "in charge" much of

---

* The divorce rate is 50 percent. The likelihood that your second marriage will end in divorce is closer to 60 percent. If you fail to give serious scrutiny to your role in a marital problem, you run the risk of repeating problems in a new marriage.

♥ ♥ ♥

BUILDING A SUCCESSFUL RELATIONSHIP

If you believe you've reached an impasse in your efforts to deal with a relationship difficulty, ask yourself, *How would my mother (or father) have handled this problem?* How did your parents deal with anger? with grief? with sexual feelings? with anxiety? If you've regarded your parents as wise and caring, imagining how they'd deal with matters can give you new ideas or help you feel comfortable with paths you've already taken.

If you have some negative views of your parents, you might find you are handling a problem similarly to a way they would have handled it—which can help you to see other alternatives. Or you might discover you try so hard *not* to act like your parents that you overlook ways of coping that might work, simply because they conform to ways your parents might have used.

Regardless, considering how your parents might handle your problem if they were in your shoes can be an eye-opening experience.

♥ ♥ ♥

the time, and Nick and Gina were no exceptions. So power struggles emerged between them. Had Nick married a woman who was the youngest in her family, they would probably fight less often (especially if her eldest sibling was a brother). Does that mean Nick and Gina are incompatible? No. Actually, both Nick and Gina would be better off letting someone else take the reins of control once in a while. That would be less likely to happen if they married someone who had no desire to take charge. The fact that Nick grew up with younger sisters and Gina grew up with younger brothers helps their relationship. They are attuned to the needs and behaviors of the opposite sex. If each had been the dominant sibling with no sibling of the opposite sex in the family, they would have an even harder time.

Keith and Sheila were also frustrated by one another. Each grew up as an only child. Only children receive much more attention from parents than do children with siblings. Consequently they are brighter and more mature for their age, and often get along better with children older than themselves. Accustomed to a lot of attention, only children may clash with one another in a marriage because each one is looking for more attention from the other than is provided.

As you can see, one's sibling position can and does make a difference. Spouses who grew up as the youngest in their families may flounder as they expect more support from one another than is able to be readily given. But youngest children do get along well as adults with a mate who was an older child.

Middle children are not as easily categorized. To some extent they learn how to get along well with older and younger siblings. They can fit in with a crowd. They make good vice-presidents. But they may be reluctant to stand out and take charge. In a very large family, those in the middle may cluster and one may emerge as the more dominant middle sibling while another might emerge as the more submissive.

Dr. Walter Toman did the original research on sibling position. Essentially he discovered that those adult relationships that were more likely to endure were relationships that perpetuated the role one had in one's former sibling position. People grow accustomed to giving orders, taking orders, asking for help, not asking for help, etc.

Four Ways to Put Your Past behind You

How can you shake loose an old pattern of relating—one that was formed in your childhood years? Well, you really don't want to abandon that role entirely. You want to be more flexible. Often, a 15-percent adjustment is enough to make matters on the home front work fine. Not perfectly, but fine.

First, stop blaming your spouse for problems that originated in your childhood. Your spouse didn't cause them. If your mate is perpetuating them, it is because you have offered aid and comfort. For example, a woman who felt rejected or abandoned as a child may be quick to doubt her spouse's commitment to her. But chances are she is overreacting. Her mistrust can then offend her mate, who over time distances himself from her.

Second, try to view your spouse as the person you married, not as the person you grew up with or were raised by. It's not always easy to do, but you owe it to your marriage to look at your mate as a unique individual with ideals, fears, and goals—some of which are miles away from experiences you had growing up. Try this exercise:

Create a picture in your mind of your mate. Get a clear, close-up image. Try to look at your mate as a stranger might. What would a stranger see? What qualities of your mate would another man or woman find attractive about your spouse? Now, look for a facial expression that reminds you of how your mate looked when you were dating. A certain expression, a certain smile . . . What hopes and dreams did that younger person possess? As you keep looking at this picture, your emotional reaction to it will modify slightly. The person you fell in love with is still there, essentially.

Now, if you have a strong negative view of your spouse—especially a view that reminds you of a parent—try seeing it as a template that overlays the image. Now lift off the template and put it aside, allowing a clearer image of your mate to emerge. Who is the person you now see?

Completing this exercise can help you to loosen some of the ground-in dirt that over the years has accumulated on the image you hold of your mate.

A third way to break away from binding past roles is to *change the role you currently play with your siblings.* If you are the oldest sibling who overruled the others, ask them for advice or assistance. Call them more frequently, but as a peer, not as their manager. Don't be afraid to admit it when you don't know something. Show enthusiasm for their successes. If there is any quality of theirs you prize or envy, tell them.

If you are a younger sibling unaccustomed to being taken seriously, now is the time to assert yourself. Inviting siblings to your place for a family barbecue can show them that *you* can take charge. If they try to help too much, don't let them. If you feel teased, speak up.

If you were (are) the family peacekeeper, resign your position. Basically, any role you feel locked into is one you need to free yourself from. Reestablishing a personal one-to-one relationship with each and every one of your siblings can be one of the more powerful things you can do to break out of old patterns.

A fourth way is to *write a letter to your parents and siblings, informing them of some of the personal changes you intend to make.* This may seem a bit extreme, but it can motivate you to persist and will help ferret out any obstacles the family might throw at you. (If they throw no obstacles in your path, you're not that stuck to begin with.) Some roles a family will be reluctant for you to give up. Tina was the family caretaker. When her widowed father was recovering from a heart attack, she was expected (and she obliged) to do anything and everything that was required to help him. She was his nurse, his accountant, his attorney, and his entertainment when he tired of television. Did her brothers help? Why should they, since she was doing it all? Eventually she became clinically depressed and was unable to help out. Her brothers were forced to enter the picture and assist their father. As her depression lifted, she wrote her family a letter and outlined her new role. She did not insist that her brothers take on more responsibilities, but she made it clear that her ability to care for her father was quite limited. In the future she would be doing far less than she had been for her father. She loved him, but she was burned out. There was a family uproar over this, initially. But they got the message, and the family repositioned itself with new, more flexible roles.

Keep in Mind

- You don't have to abandon old ways of relating. You want to add to them to enhance your flexibility.
- We often want our mate to repeat ways of relating that we found appealing in our parents, and we want our mate to change those ways of relating we found unappealing in our parents. Expectations a bit high, wouldn't you say?
- You are not doomed to replay old scripts from your earlier years. Some scripts take time to rewrite, however.
- If your marital role is similar to your sibling role, changing your old style of relating to your siblings may be easier than modifying your marriage (and just as helpful).

Part Two

Chapter 9

When Communication Is the Problem

You won't get to the heart of the matter if you can't talk things out.

Communication is not only the tool used to fix most marital problems, it can be a problem in and of itself. How do you fix a problem when the tool and the problem are one and the same? Saying to your mate, "We have a communication problem. Let's talk about it" is like giving someone who can't read a book about illiteracy. But what's a couple to do?

When couples enter a therapist's office and complain, "We don't communicate," they usually mean that one (or more) of three things happens when they try to talk matters out:

1. They literally don't communicate. Instead they withdraw, keep to themselves, and discuss matters superficially.
2. They fight. They get loud and sarcastic, or they blame, call one another names, and get nowhere.
3. They don't feel understood. The words are clear, the tone is fairly calm, the requests seem reasonable, but the message does not compute.

Communication difficulties scare and frustrate couples. You may stay with a mate who has a different point of view on spending habits or child rearing, but how can you be happy when your efforts to communicate lead to misunderstandings? In chapter 1, I explained that couples with recurrent conflicts have two general problems. Problem one is whatever issue or misunderstanding they are dealing with at the time (money, lack of time together, etc.). Problem two is the bad feelings that resulted from mishandling Problem one.

Problem two is most often a by-product of ineffective or counter-productive communication efforts. A vicious cycle develops from this. Ineffective communication prevents problem solving, which builds up bad feelings. Bad feelings accumulate and interfere with one's ability to communicate with understanding and caring. Communication is once again clogged, which prevents problem solving and adds to bad feelings, and so on.

Once this cycle repeats a few times, an unfortunate thing happens: FURTHER EFFORT TO TALK THINGS OUT MAKES MATTERS WORSE. It is like having a severe allergic reaction to medicine. The medicine is supposed to help, but it only adds to your misery. Then what do you do? Many couples give up conversation for a while. Eventually they try again but often get the same results. Then matters have gotten completely out of hand. Help!

Getting off the Not-Very-Merry-Go-Round

Raise your hand if the way you and your mate communicate is a problem. Good. Admitting that is a necessary first step. Now, raise your hand if you believe your personal skill level in communication is inadequate. Hmm. Fewer hands were raised. Okay, raise your hand if your spouse's skill level in communication could stand some improvements. Ah-ha! More hands were raised that time.

This is a common finding with couples who can't communicate: They might admit that "we" have a communication problem, but usually they believe that "he" or "she" has more of a problem than "I" do. People have talked all their lives, usually with a fair amount of success, so they are generally reluctant to acknowledge that they lack communication skills. Yet I've worked with people in sales and in the media—people who make their living communicating—who flounder when talking to their mates.

Remember how poor communication leads to poor problem solving, which leads to bad feelings, which impedes communication and interferes with problem solving—and so on? To get out of that rut it is important to do more than just improve your communication skills. You must also do something immediately to soothe the bad feelings. Why? Because the presence of bad feelings can impair your efforts to learn new communication skills. Moreover, you and your mate are bound to make mistakes while learning to communicate effectively, potentially adding to the bad feelings. If you reduce the bad feelings, you are more likely to give your partner the benefit of the doubt when he screws up in his communication skills efforts.

Soothing the Bad Feelings

1. *Apologize to your mate for your role in the communication problem.* Maybe you've apologized before, but do it again. Be sincere. A note or greeting card with the same message is a nice touch.

2. *Admit to your mate that you want to communicate differently from before.* Couples mistakenly try to improve communication by doing exactly the same thing they've always done, only more slowly or more patiently. It won't work. Something more fundamental must change. As mentioned in chapter 3, one hallmark of couples in recurrent conflict is their inner belief that they know "the truth" about an issue. They believe their perceptions to be accurate and their partner's to be inaccurate. They may give lip-service to the notion that they might misperceive events or jump to the wrong

conclusions occasionally, but secretly they believe otherwise. The "I'm right, you're wrong" attitude also exists when it comes to communicating. Each partner secretly believes that he or she *really is listening well, really is speaking courteously, and really is making reasonable demands.* It is his or her spouse who has the problem. For the sake of your relationship, abandon those secret beliefs. It is a necessary change, fundamental to resolving your communication impasses.

3. *Play by the rules. And if you make a mistake, don't justify your error as being "caused by" your mate, while at the same time viewing his errors as being caused by himself.* It is common for dissatisfied spouses to view their mate's motives more negatively, while viewing their own motives as benign or good. The odds are that your mate is trying harder than you think to make improvements and that he often says or does the wrong thing while attempting to get it right. If you convey to him that his efforts aren't strong enough, he'll be likely to feel unappreciated.

4. *Do nice, considerate things for one another to help improve the atmosphere.* Bad feelings can dissipate when you believe your mate wants you to feel better and that he is willing to try to help bring that about. Improving communication skills takes some effort. A little fun together can help improve the mood. Do things together that you used to do when dating. Do something for your mate that will make him or her feel a bit more special. Keep it up whether or not your mate reciprocates. Spouses may notice positive changes early on, but they may not believe them to be sincere or durable. It can take a minimum of one month for the changes to be truly appreciated. By then your mate may be more than willing to reciprocate, and you will believe that he or she wants to make improvements too.

Once you can trust that your mate is probably doing the best that he can and that he wants things to work out, your attitude toward him will improve. With a better attitude, you'll handle the occasional setbacks and miscommunications more effectively.

Improving Communication

Intimate communication with your mate is a balm for the bumps and bruises in life. In trying times, people usually turn to their mate to talk and find comfort. When you can say what's on your mind and believe you will be understood and accepted, marital satisfaction improves (or remains high). Couples who communicate well are also more likely to affirm one another—that is, show appreciation and give compliments. Studies show that affirmations from a spouse enhance well-being and self-esteem.

RED FLAGS

What are the signs that communication problems will eventually erupt?

- A belief by one or both parties that disagreement is destructive
- A belief by one or both parties that mind reading is expected
- Hinting instead of straightforward speech
- Expressing only what you dislike rather than expressing what you like
- Routine withdrawal from conflict or conversation
- Not taking a clear position on what you want or don't want
- Frequent interruptions
- Frequent blaming; infrequent examination of one's role in the problem
- Parents were poor communicators

♥ ♥ ♥

One major component of effective communication has less to do with what you say and more to do with how you feel inside. *It is the ability to tolerate emotional expressions by your mate.* If your spouse's emotions get hot and a bit out of control, how *you* respond is key.* When calm and collected, partners can tolerate differences of opinion. But when anger at a spouse—or even slight annoyance—crops up, good intentions and mature responses fly out the window for many couples. To aim for complete calmness is unreasonable, although many couples successfully achieve that. If resentment and hurt feelings have accrued, couples are more likely to do the wrong thing while communicating, despite efforts not to. Consequently, a more useful goal is to learn to respond effectively to a spouse's emotional reaction. Don't lose your cool because your mate momentarily lost hers. Don't give up trying because your mate gave you a frustrated, "Why am I even bothering?" look. In other words, if you want to stop playing the same old game but your spouse hits the ball over the net to you, don't hit it back.

That doesn't mean your spouse can ignore the rules of engagement while you abide by them. Ideally, each of you will make a sincere effort to follow rules of effective communication. But one of you is bound to mess up. And when that happens, you don't want the same old tennis match to resume. If you can learn to be less emotionally reactive (less annoyed, agitated, angry; engaging in less complain-

---

*Some communication efforts flounder when one spouse refuses to talk. Withdrawal from conflict or conversation is an *emotionally fueled* response. Don't confuse quietness with calmness. Studies show that people who are more quiet during discussions about areas of conflict usually have higher heart rates—a consequence of their emotional reaction to the discussion.

ing, sighing, etc.) in the face of your partner's emotional reactivity, you have a real chance to handle the rest of the discussion well. You can be less emotionally reactive if you feel more confident in your own communication skills and if you are not insistent on how your partner "should" feel or behave. Remember, if you resent your partner's actions, there is something you do not understand. Better to aim for understanding than shoot down your partner's character.

Don'ts

Communication efforts can withstand a number of broken rules. But there are some rules you want to be absolutely sure you never break. Among them:

Don't ridicule or embarrass your mate. Name calling, put-downs, and slurs on his character or background dig deep holes in your partner's heart and his memory. Even "minor" put-downs such as "I thought you were smarter than that!" can do long-lasting damage.

Don't threaten separation or divorce as a way to punish or coerce a mate. Your commitment to one another is fundamental to your marriage. Carelessly tossing it about can weaken your partner's resolve to improve matters. If you and your mate have embarked on a plan to improve your relationship, make a commitment to that plan. Don't allow a bad day to cause you to give up. Threats to separate tell your partner you are not that invested in him. He may start to give up, and a self-fulfilling process unfolds. *Understand that in dissatisfying marriages it is common to have thoughts of separation. But it is also common for those thoughts to come and go.* If you threaten separation but in reality you are *unsure,* then your threats will do more harm than good. If you're angry, say so. If you're hurt, tired, frustrated, or pessimistic, say so. But don't talk of separation unless you are ready to give very serious thought to the matter. It should never be a threat.

Don't verbally abuse your mate. Verbal abuse can be more than put-downs. It is a form of intimidation and harassment, whereby raising one's voice, criticisms, and out-shouting one another are done to coerce, punish, or control. While verbal abuse does not always lead to physical abuse, physical abuse is always preceded by verbal abuse within the relationship.

Don't use physical force. Get up and leave before you take it that far. If a partner feels threatened by your use of force, trust is gone. Agreements may be reached out of intimidation rather than constructive problem solving.

Don't punish your mate. If you want time for yourself, take it. But don't avoid your mate for days as a maneuver to punish or show how angry you are. Don't wear your partner out with your arguing or blaming. Don't refuse to attend an important function purely as a maneuver to get even. Don't sleep on the couch, don't refuse to eat meals with your mate, don't halt good-night kisses. Such actions can scar a relationship. They are actions not likely to be forgotten and may prompt your mate to find ways to punish you.

Do's

During an argument or important conversation, summarize your partner's point-of-view before you express your own viewpoint. Begin the summary with words like, *"What I hear you saying is . . ."* or, *"You're telling me that . . ."* If your summary is accurate, your mate will feel understood and listened to, and you will have slowed the conversation down to a more workable pace. If your summary is inaccurate, your mate can correct the inaccuracy. Occasional inaccurate summary statements reveal that you and your mate probably had unhelpful dialogues in the past, each mistakenly believing you understood your partner when you did not.

Request what you'd like from your mate instead of complaining about what you don't like. Arguments and misunderstandings unfold quickly when all you do is complain without being specific about what you want from your mate. Complaining, "Why must you watch TV so much?" is likely to aggravate your mate. Requesting, "I'd like us to spend more time together. How about we go for a stroll later on?" is less hostile and more to the point. Complaining without making a request will often lead to pointless debates.

"I don't watch TV that much!"

"Yes, you do."

"No, I don't."

How much he watches TV is not the issue. How much you want him to spend time with you is.

If you are tense or aggravated, asking "Why?" questions is a clue that you are probably complaining instead of making a request. *"Why can't you . . ."* or, *"Why don't you . . ."* or, *"Why must you always . . ."* are complaints, not legitimate questions. No response your spouse makes to such questions will appease you. So skip the questions and get to the heart of the matter. Say "I'd like it a lot if you would . . . Does that sound reasonable?"

Keep listening until you can validate your partner's viewpoint. You validate his view whenever you can comment on what he said that has merit. You don't have to agree with him, but you want to be able to say something like, *"Given your perspective on what happened, I can see why you felt angry."* You invalidate your spouse whenever you scowl, roll your eyes, or tell him he's wrong or foolish to think or feel a certain way. Examples of invalidating comments:

> *How can you say such a thing!*
> *You don't know what you're talking about!*
> *Oh, give me a break!*
> *You're wrong again!*

How dare you!
How could you!

Nonverbal ways to invalidate include shaking your head in disgust, rolling your eyes, sighing, turning your back, and tuning out. Certainly your partner may be wrong or hurtful, and you have a right to give your view. But remember, *most of the time people think their views do make sense and that their demands or complaints are reasonable.* If your first response is to challenge, debate, or otherwise invalidate your partner, the conversation will be unsatisfying. *Wait until you can see things from his perspective before you tell him yours.*

Make A-B-C statements. Instead of accusing, phrase your concerns this way: *"When I hear (or see) you do A, I think B, and feel C."* So the accusation "You're not listening!" can be phrased, "When I'm talking and see that you're looking at the newspaper [A], I think you don't want to listen to me [B], and I get annoyed [C]." A-B-C statements are far less accusatory and do allow your mate to understand your reasoning.

If a troublesome thought or feeling persists, don't suppress it. Address it! In her book *Lucky in Love*, author Catherine Johnson points out that happy couples may be annoyed with one another two to three times a week but are able to get over it quickly, often without comment. The key for them is their capacity to genuinely forget about it. But if an annoying feeling recurs and can't be forgotten, it needs to be addressed, not suppressed. The husband of a couple I saw recently announced that he'd been resentful for four years that his wife took a new position in her company, requiring her to travel and spend a great deal of time away from home. He particularly resented that she had never bothered to discuss her plans with him before announcing her decision. The wife was surprised. Not only did she not realize how resentful he was, she had never explained to him that her job change was as much a surprise to her as it was to him. "My manager called me in one day," she said, "and told me staff cuts were to be made. I could keep my job only if I took this new position. Since we couldn't afford to have me out of work, I accepted the position." She had never explained that scenario before, and he had never inquired. So for four years he was resentful—and unnecessarily so.

"But All This Seems So . . . Unnatural"

I suppose it does. Couples don't ordinarily speak using *summary statements* or *A-B-C statements.* But if you were learning any new skill—such as playing the piano—you would have to do things that seemed awkward and contrived (such as stretching your fingers to play certain chords). Allow yourself to feel a bit self-conscious using these techniques, but use the techniques anyway. In situations where understanding what is communicated is essential (such as a pilot speaking to the control tower), the participants use sign-off phrases such as "Roger" or "Over" to indicate that a message was received and understood. In face-to-face dialogue, people often *presume* their message has been heard and understood without knowing for sure. Sometimes their presumptions are wrong. The bottom line: If you were communicating clearly and effectively and were listening clearly and effectively, you'd have very few communication problems. Bone up on your communication skills. They can probably stand some improvement.

♥ ♥ ♥

MARRIAGE MATTERS

Why are communication clogs common? Look below at the anatomy of a conversation and see how easy it is to miscommunicate. It's more of a mystery how people ever communicate effectively, given all that could go wrong.

Anatomy of a Conversation

1. The Speaker speaks.
    A. But he must be able to say what he intends to say, and
    B. He must be able to say it in a manner that is clear.
    C. Furthermore, what he intends to say needs to convey adequately the meaning he wants to get across.
2. The Listener listens. This step is even more complicated than Step One. Assuming the Speaker was clear, the Listener must nonetheless
    A. Hear the Speaker's words and not be distracted.
    B. Interpret the words to mean what Speaker intended.
       But the interpretation will depend upon other factors. First, the Listener may interpret certain words to mean something other than what the Speaker meant. Vague phrases such as "I'm upset" or "I'll be home in a little while" will cause confusion if not clarified. Second, the Listener may have an emotional reaction to the Speaker's message (usually anger, guilt, or anxiety) which can interfere with effective listening. Third, the Listener may have an emotional response to his own emotional reaction. For example, if his emotional reaction was anger, he may be *annoyed* that he got angry or *scared* that he got angry.
    C. Listener must respond. But Listener must also be clear, saying what he intends to say.
3. The Speaker must now listen, etc.

As you can see, simple conversations are not so simple. Therefore, complicated conversations about important and previously misunderstood information must proceed using certain communication rules if the discussion is not to be derailed by conflict.

♥ ♥ ♥

Getting to the Heart of the Matter

As I mentioned at the outset of this chapter, not only do people communicate to resolve problems, communication *is the problem* for many couples. When communication efforts have repeatedly been unsuccessful, use of the four-part formula discussed in chapters 5 through 8 will be necessary.

THE FOUR-PART FORMULA

1. Unhook yourself from any emotional triangles.
2. Examine what *you* are doing (not your partner) that might be perpetuating the problem. Alter unhelpful attitudes.
3. Uncover hidden agendas.
4. Examine childhood or prerelationship events. How might they be keeping you stuck?

♥ ♥ ♥

Arthur and Diane had repetitive arguments. Efforts to discuss matters rationally always failed. Middle-aged, they moved into Diane's mother's house partly to assist Diane's mother, who was ailing, and partly to ease their own financial burdens. But Art had a history of not getting along with his mother-in-law. He viewed her as dominating and selfish. Diane understood Art's viewpoint but believed he had alienated her mother by the shabby manner in which he had treated her over the years. Diane's and Art's arguments were punctuated by name-calling, shouting matches, and walking away from one another in disgust.

Applying the Formula

Step One: Unhooking Emotional Triangles

First, Diane *Pinpointed* the Diane-Art-Mother triangle that was operating. As tension rose between Arthur and Diane, Diane's mother inevitably entered the picture. Either she literally entered the room to inquire why they were arguing or Diane and Art would mention her name in their argument. While they debated *about* Diane's mother ("You should show my mother more respect"), they were really arguing about how their own relationship was lacking in mutual respect. But as long as the mother was the topic, they didn't have to address the more fundamental concerns.

Diane and her Mom also complained to one another about Art. When Diane couldn't work out an issue with him, she'd talk to her mother instead. That was another way that Diane "triangled in" her mother.

Diane had to *Plan* how she'd dismantle the triangle. First, she unhooked herself from the triangle by refusing to allow the "mother" issue to take them away from any marital concerns that were raised. In the past, when Art complained about Diane's "exorbitant" spending habits, Diane would ordinarily mention her mother. She'd emphasize that since they were living with her mother, they needed to help out with some household expenses. Now, instead of bringing her mother up as a topic, Diane worked to keep conversations with Art only about the two of them. It wasn't easy. She began by using *summary statements* instead of automatically defending her expenditures.

"So you're really angry that I spend large sums of money without checking with you first."

"Absolutely," said Art. "Our income is limited. I feel like my financial concerns mean nothing to you."

"And you're telling me that you worry about our financial status and that it feels to you that I don't care about that."

"Yes," answered Art.

By effective use of summary statements, Diane communicated to Art *for the first time* that she listened and understood his concerns.

Sometimes Art would insist that his mother-in-law was the problem and should be discussed. But Diane always brought the conversation back to marital concerns, not just mother-in-law concerns. She wasn't always successful, but enough of the time she was.

Diane also restrained from complaining to her mother about Art. And when her mother complained to her about Art, she politely changed the topic.

After *Pinpointing* the triangle and *Planning* what to do about it, Diane *Predicted* the response she would get from Art and her Mom. She predicted that each of them would get more agitated when she first unhooked the triangle and that each would insist she act in her former manner. Her predictions were correct. Art found it difficult to discuss their marital relationship. He preferred to keep focusing on his mother-in-law. And Diane's Mom was feeling a bit alienated from Diane. She knew her son-in-law didn't like her, and she always felt closer to Diane when they both discussed how difficult Art was to live with. Now her relationship with Diane had to be founded on more than their mutual frustration with Art. But Diane *Persevered* and refused to get hooked back into the triangle.

Step Two: Examining Your Role in the Problem

Next, Diane reviewed some of the communication do's and don'ts mentioned earlier and made a list of guidelines she planned to follow during her discussions with Art. For example, she planned not to shout or put him down or interrupt him. She also planned to use summary statements frequently. She showed her list to Art and requested that he draw up his own list, which he could agree to follow.

She realized that her attitude toward Art was very negative. She believed he acted unkindly because he was mean and uncaring, while her own uncooperative behavior came out of frustration from trying to improve a bad marriage. She recognized now that she gave herself the benefit of the doubt, but not Art. She reminded herself that her communication errors and argumentative style (as well as her tendency to triangle her mother) all contributed to the current state of the relationship. And she reminded herself that many of Art's "obnoxious" behaviors reflected his *worry* that the relationship wasn't working and that *he was doing what he thought would improve the situation.* She told Art all of this. He immediately felt understood (rather than attacked) and was able to admit that his actions haven't been helping, either.

Step Three: Discovering Hidden Agendas

Next, Diane and Art presumed their arguments about money and her mother reflected deeper, hidden issues. Diane admitted that every time Art complained bitterly about her mother, she felt he had no concern for her (Diane's) feelings. Yes, Diane knew her mother could be difficult, but it wasn't easy hearing her husband complain so often. Actually, Diane had wondered for many years just how much (or little) Art cared for her. Consequently, she took a stubborn position in some arguments, hoping he'd see things her way as a demonstration of his caring.

Art's hidden agenda had to do with control. He felt his mother-in-law ruled the roost and that his role as "man of the house" was a joke. Consequently, he asserted himself and acted stubbornly as a way to exercise some influence.

Realizing all of this, Art understood that he needed to demonstrate to Diane that he could care about her. And Diane and Art saw that they needed to find ways for Art to have more say over events that involved him.

Step Four: Examining Your Past

This step was relevant for Art. He grew up believing that a man's worth had everything to do with how much money he made. Since he and Diane had financial problems, Art had been secretly feeling worthless as a man. Living with his mother-in-law because of his strained financial situation was a constant reminder to him that he had failed as a man. Understanding this helped Diane view him differently. Although she disagreed that Art's worth as a person had anything to do with income, she could see why he felt the way he did. That depth of understanding softened her view of him. He was no longer harsh and critical but a sensitive person trying hard to prop up a sagging self-esteem.

By using the four steps, Art and Diane were able to turn bad feelings into tender ones and arguments into intimate discussions.

Susan and Dick

Dick was fed up with Susan. Married for two years with no children, Dick was unable to express an opinion that differed from Sue's without being "badgered into submission. Unless I ultimately agree with her, she won't let up. She comes at me like a battering ram, insisting she's right and I'm wrong. I've had it with her."

Susan admitted as much. "I don't know why it is, but it infuriates me when he doesn't agree with me about something."

They tried talking rationally, he tried threatening divorce, but nothing changed the situation.

Susan's admission that she gets *unreasonably* infuriated, is a clue that some unconscious emotional process is fueling the fights. We proceeded using the four-step formula.

Step One: Unhooking Emotional Triangles

No triangles were evident, so we proceeded to Step Two.

Step Two: Examining Your Role in the Problem

Susan admitted that her communication style was one of beating him into submission. She took no prisoners. So she agreed to use summary statements and to speak in a quieter tone of voice. She also agreed to remain seated during discussions. (Tempers flare more when people are in a standing position.)

Dick admitted that since he had no patience with her, he sometimes disagreed with her about things she said that made sense. In other words, he got even with her by being difficult. He agreed to use summary statements and to point out aspects of her views that made sense, rather than automatically challenging her. Susan thought that would be useful for her to do too.

Step Three: Uncovering Hidden Agendas

As with most chronic conflicts, bad feelings had erupted and become the source of future conflicts. Dick made it clear he was hurt that Susan didn't seem to respect his opinion. His hidden agenda had to do with control. He didn't feel like an equal partner in the relationship, since things had to go her way.

Susan said that when Dick disagreed with her, she felt it showed he didn't care about her. She admitted that sounded foolish, but that was what she felt.

To increase Dick's sense of fairness, I recommended that if they couldn't arrive at a mutually satisfying agreement about whatever issue was at hand, they had to flip a coin and abide by the outcome. That would insure that Dick got his way 50 percent of the time.

Dick admitted that it had been a long time since he showed Susan much courtesy, let alone any genuine consideration and caring. He acknowledged that his anger at her prevented such kind actions on his part, but he realized that his lack of consideration for her only fueled her anger at him. He agreed to make a concerted effort to show her consideration—much as he would a guest in their house. So he refilled her coffee cup, asked her what she would like to do for an evening (and went along with that decision), and even gave her breakfast in bed. He wasn't overly polite, but he did try hard to show her common courtesies. It took a few weeks, but Sue did begin to feel more cared about by Dick.

Step Four: Examining Your Past

"You have such a strong emotional reaction when Dick disagrees with you," I said to Susan. "Even you agree it is a bit unreasonable. I have to think then that his disagreeing with you touches on an old issue. Was it important for you to be agreed with growing up?"

She nodded. When she was a child, evidently, her viewpoints were always discounted or made fun of—especially by her father. "If Suzy thinks it's true," her father would say, "it must be false." She had no sisters, only brothers who ridiculed her ideas. Often she'd stand up to them, particularly when her father ridiculed her mother. But it only brought her punishment. Now she has such a strong need to be validated by her husband that she can't tolerate it when he has a differing view. "And just like my father didn't care about my feelings, I get afraid that Dick doesn't care about my feelings unless he can agree with me."

Although her father and brothers had mellowed a bit, visiting her family often prompted old scripts to be recited. Sooner or later she'd give an opinion that would be mildly scoffed at by her father or brothers. Susan realized she needed to assert herself with her family. First, she sent a letter to her parents and brothers informing them how she has felt over the years. She told them they can no longer ridicule her or laugh at her ideas. And she said she'd speak to each one of them personally about this. This was not an easy step for her, but it was a necessary one. It was unfair to treat Dick as the scapegoat for her issues with her family.

It still troubled her when Dick held an opinion different from hers, but she was able to restrain herself from losing her temper. When she couldn't, Dick would gently remind her that he is not her father, that he does love her, and that he cares about what she has to say. Over the next few months matters improved even more between them.

As you can see from these two examples, it may not be necessary to use all four steps in the formula to put a halt to recurrent conflicts. You may discover, as Susan and Dick did, that one of the steps has a more powerful impact on your progress than any of the others.

You may also discover that you may have to revisit some of the steps before you can fully extricate yourself from your predicament.

Keep in Mind

- Communication is the tool to resolve all other problems. Keep it sharp and polished so it won't let you down when you need it the most.

- If you do nothing else, simply summarizing your partner's comments before you respond with your own viewpoint can dramatically improve communication effectiveness.

- Most of the time people believe that their communication attempts were clear and reasonable; so, when a communication problem crops up, there is a tendency to blame the other more than to see one's own communication flaws.

- Using communication techniques (such as making summary statements) will make you feel awkward and self-conscious at first. Don't let that cause you to give up on them prematurely.

Chapter 10

When Parenting Is the Problem

Couples in conflict over their children have primarily a marital problem, not a child problem. Yes, one of the children may be particularly difficult or troubled, and may even have been diagnosed as having attention-deficit disorder, depression, or phobias. And even if no such disorder is present, research has shown that children are born with different temperaments that can make a parent's job somewhat easier or more challenging.

Still, in this as in every area of potential trouble, how a couple *responds* to a problem is more important than the nature of the problem in determining the impact the problem will have on a couple's life. When spouses can't agree on how to discipline their children or on what's best for their children, the children are not the "disagreeable" ones in the family (no matter how difficult to manage they are).

To complicate things further, even if the parents are in full agreement about how to raise a child, a child problem may still be a marital problem in disguise. Meredith, who is twenty-nine, was always viewed by her parents as being difficult and "sassy" while growing up. She often challenged and defied her parents' rulings. Why couldn't she be like her older sister Mary? Mary was dutiful, respectful, and a good student. The fact was that underneath the family facade of mental health, Meredith's father was an alcoholic. He was the kind of alcoholic who somehow kept his job and presented an appearance of respectability, but home life was painful for Meredith and her family. Meredith's mom was often silent. She didn't like her husband's drinking, but she acted helpless in the face of it. Meredith, the "difficult child," was the warrior who fought against her dad's alcoholism. She was the visionary in the family who saw that "the emperor wore no clothes," that her family life was a mess, despite outward appearances.

"I was angry at my father for his drinking, and I was angry at my mother for her passivity."

She was frequently punished for her childhood "misdeeds"—but would you agree that she was not the problem?

Any problem in a family or in a marriage that *persists* is involved in some form of *feedback loop.* This is the phenomenon whereby one partner does X (complains), causing the other partner to do Y (withdraw), which causes the first partner to do more of X. That process is also called *circular causality.* It is likely, for instance, that Meredith's willingness to confront her father only added to his fury, making his wife feel even more helpless. Certainly his wife was never emboldened by Meredith's actions to confront him herself. Perhaps, the mother's desire to protest her husband's drinking was met vicariously by Meredith. In other words, Meredith became her voice. Consequently, Meredith's protests, which were designed to bring about change, became a force that helped maintain the status quo. In general, if a marital problem results in a child problem, the child problem can further intensify marital conflict, which can cause the child problem to persist.

In earlier chapters we saw how couples stuck in a marital rut apply failed solutions repeatedly. Rather than abandoning futile efforts, they repeat them over and over. Couples in conflict over child rearing fall prey to the same twisted logic. They presume that the culprit in the ongoing struggle is either a noncooperative child or a noncooperative spouse. Rarely do the spouses agree that the real problem is their manner of solving problems. (And if they do agree about that, each believes the other should change his or her problem-solving style.) Rarely do they examine their relationship or the emotional triangles within the family. Consequently, much effort is wasted trying to coerce one another (or a child) to "see things my way."

When a child-focused problem persists despite repeated efforts to correct it, something fundamental to the perpetuation of the problem is being overlooked or minimized.

The Family Structure

When ongoing child-related conflicts exist, it is helpful to examine the boundaries between family members and between the family and the outside world. *Boundary* is a term used to define the extent to which family members interact. If a *rigid boundary* exists, say, between father and son, then the two have little to do with one another. The father is often unaware of what is occurring in his son's life and may be lax in noticing any serious school or social problem his child might be having. Father and son may fight and argue, but there is little dialogue and an absence of intimacy. If a *diffuse boundary* exists, say between mother and son, then there is too much closeness and connection. Mother is likely to be overprotective and on edge, worried about potential problems the son may face. Son may confide in her—which to some extent is desirable—to the point of losing or underplaying his own capacity to work things out for himself. When *clear boundaries* exist, there is closeness but separateness. Each is allowed to have his or her own opinions, feelings, and preferences. Privacy is valued and respected as much as togetherness. Somewhat simplistically, knocking before entering is an indication of a clear boundary. Barging in without knocking reveals a diffuse boundary. Padlocked doors represent a rigid boundary.

♥ ♥ ♥
RED FLAGS

How can you tell when a child problem may really be a marital or personal problem? Red flags include:

- **Seeing Red.** Psychologist Ron Taffel in his book *Parenting By Heart* revealed that when a parent gets very angry over a child's misbehavior, it may be because the behavior hit a "sore spot." So a husband, offended by what he views as his wife's lack of appreciation for him, may become quite angry when his four-year-old acts ungrateful. A wife who believes her husband doesn't help enough with household chores may get into a rage at her six-year-old when he tracks mud onto the kitchen floor. The "sore spot" may also be a leftover from childhood. A man whose father was physically abusive may overreact when he sees his partner use corporal punishment.

- **Over-identifying with a child.** Some parents are convinced their child is "just like me." Ron Taffel says that when that happens, you are not seeing your child clearly. You are reacting to your child, not truly connecting. A mother who feels sorry for her daughter because the father spends little time with the child may really be reacting to her own loneliness. It is she who is upset about lack of quality time with her husband. Perhaps the girl misses her father, but Mom's identification with her daughter may complicate the picture. Her anger could further distance the father from the family.

- **Saying "I'll never be like my parents."** We only have three options as parents: to act totally like our own parents, to act totally unlike them, or to do some things similarly and some differently. When we have a strong negative emotional reaction to the way our parents raised us, we may work hard "never to be like them." But that reduces our flexibility. If you are afraid of your anger because you didn't like your parent's verbal abuse, you may become an ineffective disciplinarian. Besides, it's normal to feel angry. If your parents never gave you much, where do you draw the line when it comes to giving your children what they want? If your children begin acting exactly like your parents, chances are you have worked too hard trying to be unlike your parents.

♥ ♥ ♥

Another useful way to assess a family is to examine its *hierarchical structure.* To put it bluntly, parents should be "in charge;" children should not. Parents ideally will communicate with one another effectively about the family and its needs, and communicate with the children. Children ideally see their parents as sources of comfort, knowledge, and self-esteem. Children should have a voice in the family, but parents have the deciding vote on matters of importance. As simple as that sounds, many families cannot resolve conflicts because the hierarchy in the family is structurally unsound. It might be that one parent is disengaged from the family— on the outside looking in—or it might be that children have too much say over what happens. The most pernicious family structure occurs when one parent is overinvolved with a child and the two are aligned against the other parent. (Or a grandparent is aligned with a grandchild against the parent.) Raising children to the status of parent, or lowering parents to the status of child, makes common-sense solutions to family problems (helping a child whose grades have declined with his homework; "cheering up" a sullen child) completely ineffective.

Consider Barbara and Ryan Smith. Their concern was their daughter Sarah's declining grades in school. Barbara spoke with the teachers, took Sarah to the eye doctor, and spent hours helping her with homework. It worked, but only for a while. Ryan viewed the problem differently. He believed Sarah was lazy and watched too much television. When pressed, he blamed Barbara.

"Barbara is too involved with Sarah. Yes, Sarah isn't getting good grades, but Barbara has always fussed over Sarah in a way I think is unhealthy. Setting firmer limits is the answer."

Barbara looked hard at Ryan. To Barbara, Ryan was *underinvolved* with Sarah. He was at the office so much he rarely saw Sarah enough to grasp the full extent of her school problem. In fact, Barbara believed that if Ryan took more of an interest in Sarah, her grades would improve.

As you might have surmised, Barbara and Ryan were not that happy in their marriage. Looking at the family structure, it was clear that a diffuse boundary existed between Barbara and Sarah—that is, they were very involved with one another—while a more rigid boundary existed between Ryan and Barbara and between Ryan and Sarah—they were underinvolved.

Circular causality was operating also. The more involved Barbara was with Sarah, the more frustrated and distant Ryan became, which maintained Barbara and Sarah's closeness. Furthermore, the more unhappy Barbara was with her husband, the more she gravitated toward Sarah. And the more unhappy Ryan was with Barbara, the more he overinvolved himself with work and distanced himself from his wife and daughter. Consequently, a simple and common-sense solution, such as a tutor for Sarah or perhaps a pair of eyeglasses, didn't help much. Why? Because the problem was not within Sarah. It was within the family. Specifically, the manner in which Barbara and Ryan handled the problem kept them running in circles. The marital relationship may or may not have caused Sarah's school problem, but it was an obstacle to its resolution.

"But Shouldn't Children Add to Their Parent's Happiness?"

Well, sort of. Couples who wish to become parents probably have a rosy (and distorted) picture of the impact parenthood will have on their lives. Parenting isn't always hard work, and it can be one of the most meaningful experiences anybody can have in life. But it requires day-in, day-out effort and a lot of overtime hours, and just when you think you've got the routine figured out, the kids enter a new

BUILDING A SUCCESSFUL RELATIONSHIP

In many marriages, once children arrive, they "take over." The roles of husband and wife fade and the roles of Mommy and Daddy emerge. Eventually, parents need to strengthen their husband-wife role. Ways to beef that up include:

- Insisting on privacy in the bathroom and bedroom.

- Not allowing a child who interrupts to sidetrack you when you and your mate are talking with one another. A polite but firm "I'll talk with you when Mommy and I finish" is adequate.

- Allowing children to work their problems out with their siblings without rushing in to mediate. If they ask for your assistance, give them some guidance to resolve it among themselves. Don't automatically solve it for them. (Besides, if you always try to solve it for them, you'll become frustrated. You'll find old parental standbys like "Share!" and "Just cut it out!" emerging from your mouth—solutions that make you feel silly and really don't teach the children anything useful.)

- Not always allowing the kids to listen in on the extension when talking with your mate over the telephone. Even if the conversation is light, maintain some degree of privacy.

- Not burdening a child with your worries or problems.

- Not feeling you have to justify unpopular decisions to your children. Yes, helping them understand your rationale is fine, but you need not get defensive about it. Sometimes "Because I said so" is adequate enough.

- Being fully involved with your children when you are spending time with them. Don't try to do paperwork or other work at the same time, or you won't do well with either work or children. If children trust that you can be fully involved with them periodically, they will be more apt to give you the space you need periodically. If they are frustrated by your half-hearted attempts at involvement, they may impose themselves on you more than you like.

phase of life (kindergarten, school sports, puberty, etc.) and you have to learn to play by some new rules. To complicate matters, any discipline technique that works now will probably be less effective six months from now. And what works for one child may not for another. Parents are constantly going back and forth between cutting their kids some slack and yanking on the leash a little harder. (As a father of three, I'm tired just thinking about it.)

On the plus side, couples with children do have a lower divorce rate than couples without. In a 1985 study, researchers collected data on a large sample of couples who divorced in 1977. Regardless of education level and age when married, the length of a marriage was directly related to the number of children the couples had. In the study, *50 percent of childless couples divorced within five years of mar-*

riage, while only 12 percent of couples with one or more children did so. And couples with children usually do report that their children have made their lives much more meaningful and have given them great joy. Nevertheless, research findings are abundantly clear: Childless couples are happier in their marriages than couples with children. They are not a lot happier, but the difference is statistically significant. In fact, when you measure happiness over the lifetime of a marriage, happiness levels *peak* at two points: between the honeymoon and the birth of the first child, and after the last child has left home. What gives?

By and large, couples with children: argue more, sleep less, worry more, experience a diminishment of their sex drive (a quiet house and a hot cup of coffee become more enjoyable than sex . . .), and spend less leisure time together. Frustrated by child rearing, many parents act in ways far different from their spouse's image of them. "When we married, my wife was sweet, kind, and soft-spoken. Now when she screeches at the kids, I envision her as some wild, prehistoric animal swooping in for the kill."

Men worry more about finances when they become fathers; women worry about child care. Indeed, a main reason working mothers don't fare well on measures of well-being is that they are depressed over the struggle to find quality child care; also, they often feel their husbands don't help out as much as they could.

Younger couples today do try hard to be involved and caring parents. But if they both work, their husband-wife time loses out to parent-child time. A 1991 study in the journal *Sex Roles* examined dual-career couples with two children. From 1978 to 1988 the average woman increased her time on the job by eleven hours per week—mostly at the expense of her leisure time with her mate.

Psychologist Peter Rosenzweig, author of *Married and Alone,* writes that "when parents' obligations to themselves are continually overshadowed by attending to the children, an emotional rift between the couple is unavoidable." Unfortunately, as intimacy between spouses lessens, one or both partners usually invest even more time in the children—which only adds to the distance the spouses feel from one another.

In dual-career marriages, spouses with young children often "take turns" caring for the children so their mate can have some free time. While that is considerate and helpful, it still doesn't address the fact that the couple needs alone time *together.* And often the "free time" one spouse has is spent doing chores or shopping—things that couldn't get accomplished while caring for the kids.

Getting to the Heart of the Matter

When couple conflicts over children persist, the children are no longer the stumbling block to problem resolution. Keep in mind, it is the hurt feelings that develop as a consequence of mishandling a problem-solving effort that most undermine future success. Couples need to soothe one another's hurt feelings before making headway on the original problem.

Remember Barbara and Ryan? Their eight-year-old daughter Sarah had declining school grades. Deep down, Barbara believed that Ryan was too involved in his job (and too tired when he came home) to spend quality time with his daughter. Barbara believed that if Ryan were a more involved parent, Sarah's grades would go back up. After all, the teacher said there was no reason why Sarah couldn't do better in school, and the eye doctor said Sarah's eyes were fine.

Ryan had an opposing view. He believed Barbara pampered Sarah and let her "get away with too much"—that she hovered over Sarah, gave her no breathing room, and was too quick to help her when Sarah could just as easily do some things by herself. They were at an impasse.

Couples routinely in conflict over their children fight about two things: Either they disagree about child-rearing practices, or they accuse one another of being overinvolved or underinvolved with the kids. Ryan and Barbara fought about both those issues.

Applying the Formula

Step One: Unhooking Emotional Triangles

No question about it. Barbara, Ryan, and Sarah were stuck in an emotional triangle. Sarah's school issues, while relevant, obscured the underlying marital issues. One day in my office, Ryan stated that he and Barbara had no free time to spend together. He mentioned how at times he was available to her, but she was unavailable. And she mentioned how at times she was available to him, but he was busy doing other things. Then Ryan blurted out, "If you wouldn't spend so much unnecessary time with Sarah, we'd have time together." The gloves were off. Barbara accused, "You don't seem to care at all about Sarah. How do you expect her grades to improve if you don't take an interest?"

Do you see what they did? They had been discussing *their* relationship when they suddenly shifted the topic to Sarah. It was not a happy or gratifying topic, but it did keep them from addressing their marital concerns. *While it might seem to be common sense that if the problem with Sarah suddenly resolved itself, the couple would fight less and feel better about their marriage, the reverse is probably true: Until they can fight less and feel better about their marriage, they may never be able to resolve Sarah's problem.*

I inquired whether Sarah sometimes entered the scene when Barbara and Ryan had time to themselves. Ryan quickly pointed out how Sarah would sit next to Barbara on the couch when the couple might be discussing the events of the day. While seemingly innocuous, Sarah's presence had the effect of stifling Ryan's conversation. And the less he spoke, the more likely Barb was to focus on Sarah. The upshot? Once again the marital relationship got sidetracked.

Ryan and Barbara both agreed that they had to talk with one another about issues besides Sarah. And they agreed that they would tell Sarah to come back a little later when they were having a private conversation. Both of those objectives would unhook them from the triangle with their daughter and help them resolve their fundamental problems. But they also realized they'd have to be firm and persevere. Unhooking emotional triangles isn't as easy as it sometimes appears.

Step Two: Examining Your Role in the Problem

"If kicking the Coke machine doesn't help, kick it harder" was the rule of thumb they used when dealing with one another. For example, Ryan admitted he'd often minimize Barbara's concerns about Sarah *as a maneuver to get Barbara to reduce her overinvolvement with Sarah.* When Barbara remained concerned about Sarah, Ryan dismissed her concerns *even more.* Ryan saw how his dismissal of Barb's concerns caused her to be *more* focused on Sarah, which in turn prompted him to minimize Barbara's complaints further. His "solution" to the problem failed, but he kept reapplying it.

Barbara admitted that she'd purposely make herself unavailable to Ryan as a way to show her displeasure for his attitude about Sarah's grades. The effect of this strategy, however, was that Ryan felt more shut out and so invested more of his energy in his job instead of his family. His overinvolvement with work prompted Barbara to "punish" him more by being even less available to him, which further fueled his frustration with her. Her "solution" to the problem failed, but she kept reapplying it.

Both agreed to stop doing those things that were counter-productive and to accept responsibility for their part in the continuation of the problem.

Ryan also noted that his preferred way for dealing with conflict was to "flee." By withdrawing into his work as often as he did, Ryan now realized, he wasn't helping problems to go away but was adding to them. He agreed to make time every day for Barbara, and not allow fatigue or his job to be a convenient excuse.

Step Three: Uncovering Hidden Agendas

What were they *really* arguing about when they argued about Sarah? Their main fear was, "Is my spouse interested in me anymore? Do I matter?" When Barbara complained that Ryan was underinvolved with Sarah, she was also feeling that Ryan was underinvolved with her. Rather than work on ways to spend more time together as a couple, Barbara worked on ways to get Ryan to spend more time with Sarah. Yes, Sarah might benefit from more involvement by Ryan in her life, but Barbara was using Sarah's issue as a cover for her own issue.

And when Ryan complained that Barbara was overinvolved with Sarah, he was really complaining that Barbara was underinvolved with him. But being a "withdrawer" from conflict, Ryan had trouble articulating that. Rather than focus on ways to spend more time with Barbara (chances are, if he'd spent time with Sarah, Barbara would have felt freed up to devote more time to him), he focused on ways to get Barbara to spend less time with Sarah ("Send her to her room to do her homework").

So neither Barbara nor Ryan addressed what was truly bothering them. When couples misidentify the fundamental problem, arguments recycle.

Step Four: Examining Your Past

Barbara had to admit it. Her father was rarely available to her. She missed out on his presence and made a pact with herself that no child of hers would suffer the same fate. So when Ryan seemed to minimize Sarah's school problem and refused to help her with her homework, she saw red. "My childhood was happening all over again, right before my eyes," she said. The truth was, because of her strong feelings about her past, Barbara was not able to assess clearly all that was happening in the present. In fact, Ryan was a much more involved father than her father had been to her. When she thought about it, Sarah seemed pretty happy about her relationship with her father. Barbara had overidentified with Sarah. Simply because Barbara had certain strong feelings about her own father, she began believing that Sarah must be suffering the same way. It wasn't true. By realizing that her past was playing tricks on her vision, Barb was able to stop herself from getting carried away with her negative views of Ryan.

♥ ♥ ♥

MARRIAGE MATTERS

Being able to agree on child-rearing practices is important. Having similar values is also important, particularly when it comes to helping your teenager say "No" to sex. A 1992 study[1] of almost 1,400 students (seventh through twelfth grade) revealed that 19 percent of seventh grade students and 64 percent of twelfth-grade students had engaged in intercourse at least once.

One finding was that it didn't matter whether or not parents talked about sex with their teenager when it came to which students would be sexually active or not. "What appears to be important then is not just the communication of information, but the communication of values. . . Adolescents who thought their parents would be upset if they had sex were less likely to have sex."

Parental values were not the only factors in determining which teens had sex. Teenagers who believed that having sex was acceptable and who had friends who were sexually active were more likely than others to engage in sex.

Still, the role of parents cannot be understated. Parents have an obligation to state their values clearly to their children. Parents who disagree on standards of conduct are giving their children openings to seek out the standards of *others* in order to help them define their own.

♥ ♥ ♥

Stepparenting and Blended Families: A Special Set of Challenges

Over one-third of all children will probably be raised by a stepparent at some time in their life. While having children tends to reduce a couple's chance of divorcing, once they remarry the presence of stepchildren increases the odds that the second marriage will not survive. Within five years, about 40 percent of second marriages end up in divorce. The fact is that adjusting to new children—your stepchildren—can be a most challenging task. In a first marriage, many couples have the luxury of easing into parenthood, and they quickly learn to love their children. But in a blended family, a stepparent automatically assumes some responsibility for a child he or she hasn't had time to learn to love.

Stepfamily Problems

Numerous problems can develop in a blended family, but three tend to predominate.

1. The biological parents still war with one another, with the children caught in the crossfire. Such fighting increases the odds that the children will have a harder time adjusting to and accepting the stepparent.
2. The stepparent attempts to "make friends" with the children but is routinely rebuked.
3. The stepparent is criticized by the biological parent for the manner in which the stepparent interacts with or disciplines the stepchildren.

♥ ♥ ♥

BUILDING A SUCCESSFUL RELATIONSHIP

A stepfamily has a different set of challenges than a biological family. Here are some useful guidelines for stepfamilies, according to Emily and John Visher,[2] recognized experts:

1. The stepparent should have a say in determining the household rules. However, the stepparent should not come on in full force trying to enforce the rules.
2. The stepparent should devote a great deal of one-to-one time to each of the children. Building personal relationships can help moderate the tensions that can develop when the stepparent is together with all of the children.
3. The stepparent should not try to replace the biological parent.
4. The stepparent should explore with the children what they would like to call their stepparent.
5. Problems are best handled in family meetings.
6. Don't expect instant love. In fact, depending upon the age of the children, a stepparent may not develop the depth of love he or she might have otherwise. A stepparent may feel more love for his or her biological child than for the stepchild. However, fairness should be applied in equal doses.

♥ ♥ ♥

In some cases, all three of those patterns exist at the same time. Peggy and Ted were recently married. Ted was stepparent to Peggy's two children, who did not accept Ted's presence. At first he showed patience, but eventually Ted got angry, then grew distant. Peggy became annoyed with him for not taking a more mature attitude. Ted was unsure of his role. Should he lay down the law? Should he step back and let Peggy do all the work? Didn't he have a right to discipline the children once in a while?

When the two children were with their biological father, every other weekend, Peggy and Ted got along fabulously. But when the children returned, so did family tension.

Applying the Formula

Step One: Unhooking Emotional Triangles

In pinpointing the triangle, it became clear to Peggy and Ted that the main source of tension was between Ted and the children. When it got too tense, Peggy would enter the scene to try to defuse any explosion. The upshot was that Ted and the children didn't have an opportunity to work matters out.

Peggy and Ted agreed to let Ted handle situations where the children were challenging him or acting disrespectfully. Ted agreed he would not demand respect from the children. He would tell them he doesn't blame them for not liking the stepfamily situation. If matters get out of hand, a family meeting would be called—one that didn't exclude Ted from the proceedings.

Peggy and Ted were perceptive enough to realize that the children were probably also unhappy when with their biological father and his new wife. While Peggy and her ex-husband weren't the best of friends, neither were they enemies. Peggy made a concerted effort to keep her ex-husband informed about the children, and Ted made an effort to talk with him, too. Reassuring the children's father that Ted was a concerned stepparent who was not attempting to replace the biological father was a wise move.

Step Two: Examining Your Role in the Problem

Ted realized that the more he tried to assert authority with the children, the more Peggy got worried about the children's feelings and intervened. But the more she intervened, the more Ted felt useless and disrespected, prompting him occasionally to reassert himself with the children. Rather than Peggy's blaming Ted as immature, or Ted's viewing Peggy as taking her children's side against him, each made an effort to understand the dilemma the other was in. Peggy needed to understand that it was hard for Ted when the children were belligerent with him. And Ted needed to understand that Peggy already felt guilty about putting her children through a divorce. It was hard for her to watch them have to cope with the stepfamily living arrangement.

They agreed not to blame one another. Their situation was difficult, but it wasn't difficult because Peggy and Ted weren't trying hard enough. They were both trying hard. It just wasn't easy work.

Ted also believed that by spending more alone time with each of the children individually, he might break through some of the tension—or at least get to know the children better. So he made plans to do some fun activities with each of the children alone.

Step Three: Uncovering Hidden Agendas

Peggy sometimes wondered whether Ted could truly care about the children. Ted had underlying concerns about Peggy's loyalty to him compared to her loyalty to her children. It helped for Peggy to realize that Ted would do all he could to be a responsible stepparent, and that if his feelings for the children weren't as strong as her feelings for them, his depth of caring would be more than sufficient for a happy household. And it helped for Ted to realize that it was unfair to ask Peggy to choose between her children and him. If handled with sensitivity and understanding, any family problems would be minor and Peggy and Ted would remain together long after the children left home.

Step Four: Examining Your Past

Neither Ted nor Peggy believed that their past was interfering with their ability to make the stepfamily succeed. Ted had no history of being in a relationship where there was disloyalty. Peggy's only concern was making sure she didn't go through a second divorce. But that only made her more willing to try to handle the current family concerns in any way that would help.

Keep in Mind

- Repetitive conflicts about child-rearing practices are no longer conflicts about differences of opinion. They are conflicts over hurt feelings and a belief that the marriage bargain is no longer equitable.

- It is possible (and harmful) to be overinvolved with your children. Parents who "care too much" by overprotecting their kids are not caring as much as they think. Sometimes the most caring thing to do is back off and let your children care for themselves.

- If you are overinvolved with your children, you are underinvolved with some other important aspect of your life. If you are underinvolved with your children, you are overinvolved elsewhere. Aim for balance. Don't keep tipping the scales in one direction.

- If you had a particularly troubling period during your childhood, you may overidentify with your child when your child reaches the age you were at when your difficult time began—especially if the child is of the same sex as you.

- If you have unresolved conflicts with your parents or your mate, you will have a harder time coping with your children when they act like your parents or your mate.

- If you were a first-born child, or a child who had to take on adult responsibilities at an early age, you may have a harder time dealing with any of your children you think are pampered (such as your youngest child). And you may expect your oldest child to grow up quickly.

- The best predictor of family happiness is marital happiness. But in a blended family, the best predictor of family happiness is happiness between the children and the stepparent.

Chapter 11

When Money Is the Problem

Scott pointed to his feet. "See these sneakers I'm wearing? They're over three years old and all beat up, but I won't buy a new pair because money is tight. So do I get mad when my wife tells me she *must* buy a new bathing suit because she's tired of her other two? Damn right I get mad."

"Wait a minute, Scott," Kate interjected. "You make it sound like I don't care about our finances. I've *begged* you to buy yourself some new sneakers and clothes, but you won't budge. I make a lot of sacrifices. There are many things I'd like to buy that I don't buy. So if I decide to splurge a little and buy a new bathing suit, I think I have the right."

"Maybe I could buy some things for myself if you spent less on yourself," Scott answered.

"This is getting nowhere," Kate said.

"That's why we're here," Scott replied.

Does Arguing about Dollars Make Sense?

American couples do argue about money. Various studies reveal that, on average, about 75 percent of all couples argue about money. Doctors Pepper Schwartz and Philip Blumstein, in their book *American Couples*, revealed that money is the *primary* problem in nearly one-third of all marriages. A 1977 study by Daniel Sternberg showed that newlyweds ranked money problems as third on their list of marital woes; when interviewed one year later, those same couples ranked money problems as first. Another study revealed that for couples who divorced before the age of thirty, money was a significant reason for the failed marriage in 80 percent of the cases.

Does more money make couples happier? Not really. Certainly couples who barely get by on their income have more stresses associated with their financial situation. But generally speaking, making more money won't improve marital happiness. Most people would like more money. Most believe they could be content with just a little more than what they are currently making—which is another way of saying that most people are dissatisfied with their income. But couples who argue about money don't argue about income per se. They argue about spending. And they don't typically argue about necessary and obvious expenses such as mortgage and car payments and the fuel bill. They argue about how *discretionary income* is spent.

Like their sex life, a couple's financial life is not an easy topic for them to discuss. Newlyweds are too caught up in just being married to fight much over money. If a young couple agrees they'd like to buy a house or raise a family some day, there is often an implicit contract to save money. But if one spouse spends too much on "unnecessary items," arguments can develop.

Reasons for Money Problems

Anne Marshall Christner, in a 1990 article in the *Brown University Family Therapy Letter*, lists four main reasons why money can be a problem for couples:

1. Economic trends. When the country is in a recession or when a spouse gets laid off from work, money is a big concern.
2. Unforeseen emergencies. A car that's gone bust, a need for a new roof on your house, or a physical disability resulting from an accident can send some couples over the financial edge.
3. Ignorance. Some couples don't know enough to invest wisely. It can be hard for a couple to imagine what a college education might cost twenty years in the future. Some people are underinsured because they never really gave the matter much thought.
4. Chronic mismanagement of money. Some people can't settle for the basic Chevy—even though it's all they can afford. They must have the more expensive luxury sedan. Some parents overindulge their children, buying them expensive designer clothes and exotic computer games. Some couples routinely take the kids to a fast-food restaurant because it's convenient—easily spending ten to twenty dollars per visit. But they scramble to find enough money for Christmas presents.

♥ ♥ ♥

RED FLAGS

Money may become a divisive issue in your marriage

- If there is a sudden change for the worse in your economic standing
- If one of you tends to be secretive about your spending habits
- If one of you feels in a one-down position in the marriage
- If your parents argued frequently about money
- If you are unhappy and spend money to cheer yourself up
- If sharing in financial decisions makes you feel less in control
- If you are just getting by, financially

♥ ♥ ♥

Economic trends are not controllable by a couple. A couple can plan for emergencies, but they do not usually have enough in savings to cover any major catastrophe. But couples can become more informed about sound financial practices and can learn to manage their money more effectively. Still, spending habits remain a hot topic for many couples. How come?

It's important to understand that money (earning it and spending it) can mean different things to people. In our culture, money is often tied to the following:

- Power and control. Whoever runs the finances in any family has a great deal of power and say-so. Some spouses, because of their personality styles, insist on having as much financial control as possible. Commonly, such people can get overwhelmed with their financial concerns yet be reluctant to let their spouses take on any of the burden of money management. Giving up control is not easy.

- Self-esteem. People feel better about themselves when they get a promotion or earn more money. (Many a man will look at the man sitting next to him and wonder, *Is his wallet bigger than mine?*) In a study by Lewis Yablonsky in his book *The Emotional Meaning of Money,* he reports that the sex drive of males involved in the stock market went up as the market went up. When the market went down, there was a higher-than-usual incidence of sexual problems. Sexual potency and fiscal performance are related.

    It should be noted that the relationship between earnings and self-esteem is not as strong for women. Women have been raised to put relationships at the center of their lives, while men still regard "providing for the family" as perhaps their primary role. Still, many people—women included—see income as a way to feel superior to their family and friends. Spending money on luxury items gives them pleasure primarily because they feel superior to those who cannot afford those items.

- Love. Psychiatrist William Betcher notes how money can be a symbol and a substitute for love. Parents or spouses who have difficulty expressing emotion directly may buy things for their beloved. Dr. Betcher points out that the capacity of a couple to manage money is closely related to their capacity for love. Such things as mature giving and receiving, looking at things from the other's viewpoint, and balancing mutual needs are important considerations in both love and money.

- Comfort. Many people spend as a way to comfort themselves. Feeling blue? Go buy something. Although this practice is not harmful in moderation, it can become addictive. The pattern is similar to that of the person who must have a drink after work to relax. In each case, the person is probably a bit depressed or agitated, and somewhat dissatisfied with the current lifestyle. Doing something to improve the lifestyle is the better solution.

What money-management approach works best for couples? Actually, there are only three basic ways:

1. One spouse handles all financial matters and decisions.
2. Each share in decisions.
3. Each has his and her own account and they operate independently of one another (but split the bills).

The bottom line? Unless each spouse believes he or she has equal say over financial decisions, money cannot buy that couple contentment. Even if one spouse earns substantially less than the other (some researchers might say, *especially if one spouse earns substantially less*), the financial decisionmaking process must be equitable for a couple to get along. Since one partner cannot out-vote the other in an equitable relationship, the couple must find ways to accommodate each other's needs and wishes in a manner than is mutually satisfying. That isn't always easy.

If there is another rule of thumb for couples when it comes to successful money management, it is that spouses do well with some degree of *private, discretionary spending*. That is not to say that spouses should spend money they don't have. Neither am I saying that spouses should be secretive about their spending—they shouldn't. But spouses should be able to spend some amount of money without feeling they have to check in with their mate first. For most couples, this amounts to the freedom to buy themselves lunch, some small clothing items, a new CD, a novel, and so on without feeling guilty or irresponsible. For couples who can afford it, this freedom often extends to some costlier items such as a new suit or dress. Bigger-ticket items (a new TV) or items that one's partner might use or have an opinion about (a car, a new bed) are best discussed and mutually agreed upon.

To be fair, some spouses prefer that their mate make all the decisions about money. They have no problem with having little or no say over financial matters. However, for a couple to be happy, each spouse must believe that there is fairness in the relationship overall. Consequently, if one spouse controls one aspect of their life, it is not unusual for the other spouse to control another aspect. For example, a common finding is that if one partner is in charge of the money, the other is in charge of sex. The old saying, "You get what you pay for," is never more true than in these kinds of marriages.

A Matter of Value

The value of an object is subjective and often reflects the values a person holds. If you're an art lover, you may agree that a Van Gogh is worth tens of millions of dollars. If you thoroughly enjoy music, it may come as no surprise to discover that much of your discretionary income was spent on CDs or concert tickets last year. If you purchase a fancy car you didn't need, it might mean that social status is important to you. If you have a weekly hair appointment, your appearance matters a great deal to you.

Opinions about money management do reflect the values of each spouse. Some people are savers. They resist spending whenever they can. They say they know the value of a dollar, and they probably do, but they may not understand the value of enjoying some of the things life has to offer. Some people have little care for how much they earn. One artist I know is content to earn enough money to afford an apartment, a car, food, and materials for her work. That's it. She rarely thinks about investing, new furniture, restaurants, or whether she'll be able to afford her car payments six months from now. But she's content to live that way.

If you were given a large sum of money tomorrow—perhaps from an inheritance—how would you want to spend it? Imagine that it's not enough money to cause you to retire but more than enough to allow you to do what you've always wanted to do. How would you spend it? And how would your spouse spend it? Chances are your answer will reflect a fundamental value about money and life. Would you give some of it away? Would you invest most of it and get on with your life as it has ordinarily been? Clarifying your values may help you to understand why you and your mate argue about money. You may simply wish to spend money on items your mate sees as worthless, while he spends money on items you have no interest in.

♥ ♥ ♥

MARRIAGE MATTERS

Psychologist Philip Guerin and colleagues suggest that the following guidelines be used for couples attempting to resolve money problems:[2]

1. Money acquired by a person prior to marriage belongs to that person unless negotiated otherwise.

2. Money earned by either spouse during the marriage belongs equally to both spouses, unless otherwise negotiated prior to the marriage.

3. Unless otherwise agreed, money inherited by one spouse during the course of the marriage belongs to that spouse.

4. Children are the financial responsibility of the biological parents, even if a step-parent is wealthy.

♥ ♥ ♥

Getting to the Heart of the Matter

Financial crises, personality differences, and spending habits can combine to create conflict for couples around the issue of money. But when a solution doesn't fall into place easily, tension will rise and the likelihood of blaming increases. Once the discussion gets that personal, and once the partners develop tunnel vision (defining the problem in a very narrow way), bad feelings will develop. When that happens, conflicts about money will keep coming back like a bad penny.

Remember Scott and Kate? Scott's sneakers were worn thin, but he refused to buy a new pair because money was tight. And he resented it when Kate wanted to buy herself another new bathing suit. That wasn't the only time they argued about money. Kate frequently had to beg Scott when she wanted to buy "necessary items" that Scott didn't think were necessary. True, they didn't have a lot of money to spare, but Kate believed that Scott was completely unreasonable. "If he had his way, we would never buy anything new." "But if she had her way," Scott interjected, "we'd be in the poorhouse by now. Not a week goes by when she doesn't tell me we *must* buy something I honestly believe we can do without."

To complicate matters, when one of the children wanted something for school—a new outfit, or a backpack—Kate would sigh and say in a frustrated tone, "You'll have to get permission from your father." What she was really communicating to the children was, *Your father is cheap and it's his fault if you can't get what you want.* Scott resented that. But when he told the kids no to some request, he'd often imply that they couldn't afford it because their mother spent too much money on unnecessary items. Kate resented that. (If they each had a nickel for every time they annoyed one another about money . . .)

Applying the Formula

Step One: Unhooking Emotional Triangles

Trying to get the children to take sides in their battle over spending didn't help Kate and Scott's problem. It worsened it by adding to their mutual resentment. Besides, the problem was marital and would only be successfully resolved between Kate and Scott, not between those two and the children.

The couple agreed that getting the children involved wasn't the right thing to do. But what would Kate say to the kids if they asked to buy something? If she said no, the kids might still blame Dad, even though Kate didn't subtly blame him. And if she said yes, Scott might think she was still using the kids as her excuse to chip away at Scott's controlling nature. And what would Scott say to the kids if they asked him about buying something? Well, the truth was the kids *never* went to Scott unless they absolutely had to. They knew his answer would be "No."

The couple agreed to tell the children that they were trying to work out a more satisfying approach to money matters. Kate told them that Scott wasn't always being cheap and that sometimes his decisions were wise. Scott told them that Kate did have a better knowledge of what was "necessary" to buy and that often her decisions were wise. The purpose of saying these things was to unhook the children from their tendency to side with one of their parents against the other.

Step Two: Examining Your Role in the Problem

The cat was out of the bag. Scott admitted that at times he might have agreed to some spending request but didn't because he was frustrated that Kate never took his money concerns seriously. And Kate admitted that she'd sometimes insist some item was essential—when she knew it wasn't—because she was frustrated by Scott's unbending position. In other words, each took a more radical position as a way to protest the other's radical position—a "solution" that obviously backfired.

"I was afraid to cooperate," said Scott "because I thought if I started agreeing to her purchase requests, I'd open the floodgates. She'd wipe us out!"

"And I was afraid to cooperate with Scott," Kate said. "I told myself, 'Look what you have to go through to get just a few spending privileges. If you back down and let Scott have his way, you'll never get to buy anything.'"

Ironically, there was another scenario they had never considered: If Scott would cooperate more with Kate, she'd be less insistent on buying things out of protest. And if Kate cooperated more with Scott, he'd be less insistent on putting a nix on spending.

So the couple agreed to try and see things more from their mate's point of view. Kate would say "no" more often to spending requests and Scott would say "yes." To halt the bickering that might still occur, they also agreed that if they couldn't come to a mutually satisfying decision about some spending request, they would decide the outcome by the flip of a coin.[1] That way each could be assured of getting his or her way 50 percent of the time without the bad feelings that accompany conflict. The rule was, once an argument replaces a discussion, the coin must be flipped.

Last, Scott and Kate acknowledged that each had developed a view of the other that was more and more negative. In the past Scott had always appreciated what a good mother Kate was to their children, but that was no longer something he'd remind himself about. Kate knew that Scott had a kind heart, but frankly she'd overlooked that for a while. I explained that when couples argue repeatedly over some issue, the heat from that conflict can sometimes cause them to turn their backs and not see their partner's good qualities. Reminding themselves of their mate's positive qualities helped them keep their perspective.

Step Three: Uncovering Hidden Agendas

Were they always fighting about money when they fought about money? No. Money had come to symbolize something deeper. For Scott, his underlying issue was the need for control. Giving up control made him feel out of control. He used his own brand of logic to rationalize his views on spending, but it all boiled down to the fact that he wanted to have final say over money matters. Period. Like many people with control issues, his life became more complicated when he tried to take too much control. Kate resented being manipulated.

Kate's underlying issue was one of caring. Did Scott truly care about her feelings? If so, how could he be so damned unreasonable?

Scott agreed he needed to cut back on his controlling ways. It wouldn't be easy, and he wanted Kate to "bear with me." Kate said that she needed some indication that Scott really cared about her. They rarely did anything together anymore—certainly not those things that she enjoys (such as bird watching). Scott agreed to demonstrate more caring, and they planned to go out more together.

Step Four: Examining Your Past

I knew Scott would have difficulty loosening up his need for control. I suspected that his past was a major factor and I was right. Scott's father had died suddenly when Scott was fourteen. Being the oldest child, he took on the responsibilities as "man of the house." Money was tight, and his mother had to earn a living selling dresses. Scott became aware of the family's financial situation and often had to say "no" to his younger siblings while his mother was at work. All money was spent on "necessities"—food, basic clothing, and shelter. (Scott never could understand why designer jeans were a "necessity" for his twelve-year-old daughter.) The method he used to cope with his current family's finances was the same he had learned when he was a teenager—even though his current family was in a much better financial position.

Kate's family background also influenced her view of money. Unlike Scott, who was the oldest and used to control, Kate was second-oldest in a family of five children. She too had had responsibilities to care for her younger siblings, but she had never had the authority that her older sister enjoyed. Indeed her older sister often ordered her around. That frustrated her. For Kate, it was important to have "mad money"—money she could spend as she wished without being accountable. She was always accountable growing up.

So Kate and Scott had divergent background experiences, which complicated their conflicts over money. For Kate to have "mad money," Scott would have to give up control.

But they agreed. Kate felt that fifty dollars a week for her to spend or save as she saw fit—money that did not contribute to "necessary" items—would be acceptable. Scott reluctantly agreed. Kate agreed to lower the amount to thirty dollars if Scott would spend twenty dollars of his own "mad money." Scott couldn't imagine spending that much, but he did agree to buy a good-quality pair of sneakers.

When Scott revealed that he still looked after his mother's finances for her, I asked whether he'd be willing to share some of that responsibility with his siblings. It was a big change for Scott, but one we all agreed might help him loosen up his rigid approach to money management.

BUILDING A SUCCESSFUL RELATIONSHIP

Most couples tend to take one another for granted and, consequently, show less appreciation than they should. This is often particularly true for couples who argue about money. Especially if there is an underlying issue of control, spouses are disinclined to express gratitude, partly because saying "Thanks" can feel like being in a one-down position. Also, spouses who feel unfairly treated when it comes to spending money are less apt to express gratitude when their mate does something considerate. Why? Because they already feel their partner "owes them," so why should they offer thanks for something they deserve anyway?

If you've been battling about money, gratitude has been undernourished in the relationship. Make a pact that for a few weeks you will each express gratitude daily for something your mate has said or done. After that, try to show appreciation as often as possible. If you fight about money, showing gratitude is one of the best investments you can make in your marriage. It pays dividends and it costs nothing.

♥ ♥ ♥

Keep in Mind

- Repetitive arguments about money are not about money. Usually they are about trust and control.

- Want your marriage to grow and build equity? Then "equitable" decision making when it comes to finances is essential.

- Do you and your mate each have some private, discretionary spending (that need not be accounted for)? If so, give yourselves credit.

- Will conflicts about money management disappear if your income goes up? Don't bank on it. Most people eventually live (and spend) according to their means—which means it's only a matter of time before money arguments resume.

Chapter 12

When In-Laws and Parents Are the Problem

"My wife spends too much time with her mother."

"My husband doesn't get along with his parents, but he expects me to invite them for lunch once a week—while he plays golf!"

"In my parents' eyes, I'm not quite good enough. So I spend as little time with them as possible."

"I've always been close to my parents. My wife will just have to accept that. It's not that she doesn't come first, but I feel I owe my parents something other than giving them grandchildren."

It is safe to say that if a married person is underinvolved or emotionally distant from his parents, of if he is overinvolved with his parents and hasn't really separated psychologically from them, marital problems will eventually develop and persist.

The truth is, whether overinvolved or underinvolved, such a person is still psychologically attached to a parent—out of anger, fear, or guilt—and consequently has less psychological energy to devote to the marriage.

If a person is working to resolve any lingering issues with her parents, and if the spouse is supportive of that, it is quite possible that the marriage may grow closer. Nevertheless, it is by and large true that unresolved issues with one's parents show up as over-or underinvolvement with them (sometimes it ping pongs back and forth), with the marriage getting the backwash.

In the best of all worlds, a child grows to adulthood with a reasonably strong self-image, a healthy capacity for self-reliance, and a capability for intimacy and interdependence.

Too much independence suggests a fear of closeness. Too much dependence suggests a fear of abandonment. Each reflects a fear of being seen for who you really are. (The independent person is afraid her need for dependence will show; the dependent person is afraid her independent side will show. The independent person remains aloof so as to protect her sense of self; the dependent person gets close to gain a better sense of self.)

Independent (the better term is *overdetached*) people are viewed as strong. Dependent (*overattached*) people are viewed as weak. Actually, both are wounded. And both lack the *flexibility* required to bring about a satisfying interpersonal relationship.

A closer look at the overdetached and overattached person reveals that both are reacting to their parents. They are trying to get distant from them, or trying to get closer—even though at first glance they simply appear to be reacting to their spouses, their bosses, their children, or some other significant figure in their life.

In a healthy relationship, adult children are involved—to some extent—in their parent's lives. There is genuine caring and affection. There are periodic visits, more or less depending upon the distance in miles between them. The adult children do not get in the middle of their parent's relationship. They do not unite with one parent against the other. And the parents show caring to their adult children, but stand back and let them live their own lives. In the best of all worlds, the adult children don't view their parents as intrusive and the parents don't view their children as ungrateful.

For healthy adult functioning, spouses are more devoted to one another than to their parents. In a crisis there may necessarily be more attention paid to a parent than a spouse, but overall the marital relationship must be given priority over the parent/adult child relationship.

Like the rules of chess, it all sounds so straightforward and yet can become so complicated.

The Parent Connection

If you haven't worked out your issues with your parents and are too distant or too attached, a number of consequences can occur:

1. Overinvolvement with your parents can make your spouse feel left out.

2. Conflict with your parents can raise your expectations of your spouse. You may expect him to "make up" for what your parents didn't provide.

3. If your spouse is too close to, or too distant from, his parents, you could get caught in the middle. His parents may blame you for his distance, or may accuse you of trying to pull him away from them.

4. If you are cut off emotionally from your parents, you will probably be attracted to a person who is close to his or her family. But eventually you'll think she is too close to them, and conflict will develop.

5. If you want distance from your parents but feel guilty about it, you may expect your spouse to fill the gap between you and your folks. (Does your spouse do most of the phone calling, letter writing, and birthday greetings to your parents? Then she is in the line of fire.)

6. If you are too dependent on your parents, your spouse may try to reel you back, creating loyalty conflicts.

Except for extremes, it is difficult to say how much time spent with a parent indicates too much involvement or too little. I've known people who maintain daily contact with their parents—which may seem like a lot of time to some—and have a very healthy relationship with them. I've known couples who speak to their parents once a week who have a very unhealthy relationship. The key is not the amount of time. It is the amount of anxiety or emotional reactivity (anger, guilt, depression) one feels when dealing with one's parents (or contemplating dealing with them). The more emotional you are, the more automatic or "knee-jerk" your feelings are, the more your parents push your buttons, the more ill-at-ease you feel in your parent's presence—then the more "hooked" you are.

So when in-laws become the source of conflict for a couple, it is usually not a simple matter of "Your mother is a busybody." In-law problems don't become marital problems that easily. Rather, the couple is mishandling the in-law problem—in effect, making it worse. And in all likelihood, there was unfinished business with the parents that is now playing out in the marriage arena.

RED FLAGS

In-law issues will be likely to emerge if

- You are too dependent on your parents (emotionally or materially).
- You are cut-off from your parents.
- At least one of your parents is adamantly against your current relationship.
- Your family demands strict loyalty (and expects that your relationship with them will take priority over your relationship with your mate).
- You get caught in the middle between your parents and their conflicts.
- You have been the family "caretaker" or "rescuer."
- Your spouse cannot accept that you have some degree of loyalty to your family.
- You try to remain neutral in conflicts between your spouse and your parents. (Rule of thumb: don't take sides against your spouse.)

♥ ♥ ♥

The Sandwich Generation

Sometimes the problems that in-laws or parents pose for a couple have little to do with dysfunctional relationship patterns. The simple fact is that fifty million Americans now entering middle-age have to cope with some unique demands. Called the "Sandwich Generation," many people are caught between caring for aged and ill parents and caring for their children. Not to mention that they must care for themselves, their more frequent "aches and pains," and their "mid-life crisis," along with the taxes, the car payments, the mortgage, and a marriage that has lapsed into a coma.

Americans do not abandon their elderly parents. The vast majority of elderly· live near or with relatives or a spouse, often in a multi-generational household. According to Leslie Feinhauer and colleagues at the University of Utah, no more than 5 percent of the nation's elderly live in institutions.

Studies show that caregivers of Alzheimer's patients had an immune system that weakened over time. But it isn't just the stress per se of trying to care for someone with a chronic illness that weakens people. A key ingredient is the perception of *loss of control*. In fact, many middle-aged caregivers do feel their life has spun out of control. Caring for a parent with a chronic and debilitating illness prompts people to give up aspects of their lives that once were pleasurable and rejuvenating. And they often have to put other important parts of their lives—their family, their job, their own health—on the back burner. A 1992 study in the journal *The Gerontologist* revealed that in caring for a relative with Alzheimer's Disease, caretakers lose or give up aspects of themselves and become "engulfed" in the life of the ill person. *Women caregivers lost more of a sense of self than did men.* The greater the demands on the caregivers, the stronger the engulfment. Caregivers who had identities other than as helper-to-others (parent, professional, close friend, etc.) and maintained their ties to those identities fared better than those with fewer identities.

In a crisis, you might have to drop everything to help a parent or in-law. But if that person's problem becomes chronic, or if the difficulty will simply take a long time to subside, you must take a different approach—otherwise your efforts to help them can end up unraveling your own life. The following guidelines can help when you must care for an elderly parent or in-law:

- Maintain as many of your hobbies or leisure activities as possible. Don't neglect your need for replenishment.

- Delegate as much responsibility as possible to other adults in the family. If others will not cooperate, don't take on extra burdens that you cannot maintain over the long haul. It is better to be clear about your limits now than three months from now when you are exhausted and resentful.

- Don't be reluctant to hire or arrange for a home health aid or nurse. The "patient" may protest—preferring that you be the primary caregiver—but you do have leverage. Keep in mind, that what seems reasonable for you to take on as a responsibility right now can be a totally unreasonable burden six months later. Plan ahead.

- If you say "yes" when you'd rather say "no," you are hurting yourself and will build resentment.

- If you are caring for an in-law, you will resent it if you don't believe your spouse is doing his or her fair share. Once resentment emerges, talk it over with your spouse until you reach a mutually satisfying agreement.

- If you are caring for your parent, your spouse may resent the time you spend away from home and from him. Criticizing him for that won't help. Better to validate his feelings ("I know it hasn't been easy on you either"), and discuss ways to build closeness during this time.

- Feel free to designate some times during the day as your "off-duty" time. For example, you can request that your parent or in-law not make demands upon you during the dinner hour or after nine p.m., unless it is urgent.

Caregivers usually fall under the weight of their burden when they do two things:

1. They take on more responsibility than they can reasonably handle.
2. They are more invested in helping the parent or in-law than that person is willing to help him or herself.

The moral of the story is, set limits for yourself, stick to them as much as possible, and don't offer to do things that the other person can be reasonably expected to do for herself.

Getting to the Heart of the Matter

Regina had big problems with her mother-in-law. Through the years their relationship was polite, but Regina often felt criticized. Ironically, her husband was often praised by his mother despite the fact that it was Regina who most often called her, sent her birthday cards, and invited her for Sunday dinner. Matters worsened after Regina's mother-in-law had back surgery and required extended home care. Regina offered to help out by bringing meals to her in-laws and driving her mother-in-law to various doctor's appointments. But it quickly grew into more than that. She was soon doing their laundry. (Her father-in-law pleaded ignorance and his wife agreed he was not good at such chores.) The mother-in-law insisted that some doctor's appointments be made at times convenient for *her*, not at times convenient for Regina. Regina would receive phone calls from her mother-in-law complaining that Regina wasn't doing enough.

Part of the problem was Regina. She had always been a "placator," someone who'd rather appease than provoke. And she often felt guilty when she had to turn down a request for help. But where was her husband Phil in all this? Nowhere to be seen. Phil had never really had a close relationship with his mother (*I wonder why?*), and basically he allowed Regina to stand in for him as next-of-kin. Regina asked Phil for help with his mother. He complied, but grudgingly. Often he'd tell Regina not to take his mother's criticisms personally ("She's always been like that. It's not your fault"), yet he expected her to assist his mother in her recovery. When Regina came to my office she was feeling depressed and anxious. *"Would Valium help?"* she wondered.

Applying the Formula

Step One: Unhooking Emotional Triangles

Regina was in several triangles:

1. Regina, mother-in-law, Phil
2. Regina, mother-in-law, father-in-law
3. Regina, mother-in-law, mother's-in-law's symptoms

In essence, whenever mother-in-law had trouble with her symptoms, her husband, or her son, Regina became the object of focus. As is typical for people trapped in the middle between others and their conflicts, the middle person absorbs much of the anxiety for the system. (Someone who enters therapy with depression or anxiety is frequently the *strongest* person in the family. He or she simply took on too much responsibility for the problems between other people. When the symptoms of the middle person subside, symptoms or conflicts develop in the other members of the system as long as the middle person no longer absorbs their problems for them.)

Regina was no longer going to be the sponge for other people's problems. She still assisted her mother-in-law, but only under her own terms. If her mother-in-law complained, Regina politely responded, "I'm sorry you feel that way" and gave no other explanation. If pushed, Regina told her mother-in-law, "Sounds like you should be talking about that with your son (or your husband)." If her mother-in-law phoned to complain, she'd give the phone to Phil. If she complained to Regina in person or phoned when Phil wasn't at home, Regina would stop what she was doing and write out her mother-in-law's complaints and hand them to Phil when he arrived home. Regina was not going to argue with her mother-in-law. She simply refused to react in her typical way with the woman.

Regina predicted that such an approach would cause her mother-in-law to "stroke out." She anticipated that her husband—and even her father-in-law— would give her a hard time. She understood, however, that reacting emotionally to those complaints from the others—while understandable—would only keep her emotionally hooked at a time when she was attempting to detach herself from the situation. (The goal of anybody who is trying to unhook herself from a triangle is to do so with little guilt, anger, or anxiety. The more emotional a person is at that time, the less she will be able to unhook herself.) So Regina rehearsed, responding to her husband with phrases like, "I know this isn't easy for you" or "I'm sorry to hear that."

Step Two: Examining Your Role in the Problem

Regina was clear that her concern about being liked and her tendency to feel guilty if she took care of her own needs was a major part of this ongoing problem. She recognized that in a conflict situation, her tendency was to *fold*. She'd submit and give in, rather than stand up for herself or risk a confrontation. *Folding* is the conflict style most associated with depression. Regina knew that to overcome her depression she had to believe that her feelings mattered and that she had rights.

Phil was reluctant to admit that he played a role in this problem. He believed that Regina simply overreacted to his mother and should learn to say "no" once in a while. He explained his reduced (minimal?) involvement with his mother as a function of his work schedule. He was too busy and too tired. Regina said she was too, and that she therefore planned to do less for his mother. Slowly Phil realized that he used Regina as a conduit between his mother and him. He had little choice now but to increase his involvement with his mother.

Step Three: Uncovering Hidden Agendas

For quite some time Regina had felt that her relationship with Phil was inequitable. He called the shots and she obeyed. They had never argued about that before, and Regina was never fully aware of her resentment at Phil. Now she was more aware, and the couple had the opportunity to reshape their relationship so that it felt more fair to Regina. She wanted to return to school. That meant Phil would have to run the household while she was studying or in class. And it meant the kids would have to help more with chores.

Step Four: Examining Your Past

At this point, neither Phil nor Regina felt it was necessary to explore their backgrounds. While past issues may have played a role in the way their problems with Phil's mother developed, they believed they had a handle on the current situation and an effective plan to cope with it. They understood that if problems recycled, they'd have to take a closer look at their own childhood backgrounds to help them halt the problems once and for all.

Keep in Mind

- If you are overattached or underattached to your parents, your expectations of your spouse are distorted and marital problems will be likely to develop.

- The more unsettled issues you have with your parents, the less capacity you have for dealing straightforwardly with marital concerns.

- Stand up for your spouse if your family finds fault with him or her.
- If you are a caregiver for a parent or in-law, don't assist them in things they can reasonably be expected to do for themselves. You have too much to do as it is, and the parent will benefit from controlling aspects of his or her own life.

BUILDING A SUCCESSFUL RELATIONSHIP

When attempting to resolve in-law problems, the following guidelines will help:

- There must be some tolerance for the fact that each spouse will differ somewhat in the amount of contact they wish to have with their parents. There is no absolute "right" amount of time.
- Each spouse should take responsibility for dealing with his or her own family on problematic issues. Each spouse should make a concerted effort to get along with his or her parents. Set limits where appropriate.
- Marital bonding should take precedence over bonding with a parent or in-law.
- Never openly take sides against your spouse. Hash out your disagreements in private. If you feel that to be loyal to your parents or family-of-origin you must be disloyal to your mate, choose loyalty to your mate.
- Allow in-laws to be emotionally reactive when you try to unhook yourself from a triangle with them. But work at not being emotionally reactive to their emotional reactivity.
- If you vehemently oppose your mate's involvement with her family, you may have reason to be upset. But chances are you have insecurities about yourself or your marriage that you haven't really addressed. By focusing on your in-laws, you are avoiding more fundamental issues within yourself and your marriage.

♥ ♥ ♥

Chapter 13

When Sex Is the Problem

Celeste was worried. Her marriage seemed like a good one but she often found excuses to avoid sex. Her husband Don read in a magazine about something called "Inhibited Sexual Desire," and thought Celeste should get some professional help.

The first meeting in therapy shed little light on the subject. Don and Celeste spoke about their three years together and how everything else in their marriage was fine. Except sex. He was always eager, she wasn't. No obvious reasons why emerged from the meeting. The next day Celeste phoned me. She said she was too embarrassed to speak openly at our session but wanted to alert me to a concern of hers. Celeste revealed that when having intercourse she rarely reached orgasm, but was able to reach orgasm easily while masturbating. She was afraid that perhaps that meant she was subconsciously turned off by Don. Could that be?

"Did you know," I said to Celeste, "that the time it takes a man to reach orgasm during masturbation is about as long as it takes a woman to achieve orgasm? But that during intercourse, it takes women *longer* to reach orgasm?"

"I never knew that," Celeste admitted.

I explained that without adequate clitoral stimulation, many women won't reach orgasm. Intercourse alone may not always be sufficient. And typically, women achieve orgasm while making love only about half the time.

Celeste called several days later to cancel their next appointment. Once she realized that her "problem" was not a problem, she had relaxed and enjoyed sex with Don for the first time in almost two years.

Misinformation about sex had caused Celeste to draw the wrong conclusion about her sexual functioning. Worrying that she and Don might not be compatible, she avoided sex (much as someone might avoid talking about a problem for fear of making it worse). As a result, Don became frustrated, adding to the tension Celeste already felt. But the more anxious she became, the more her sexual desires lessened—which only fueled her secret worry that there must be something fundamentally wrong with her or her marriage.

In other words, as with most couples with a persistent problem, Celeste's "solution" to her inhibited sexual desire (which was to avoid sex with Don and masturbate more), only added to her fears and made the problem worse.

Jack had a different problem. Married for sixteen years, he was head-over-heels intoxicated with the woman who worked down the hall from him. If she was aware of his feelings, she didn't let on. But the sound of her voice, the mere sight of her from far away, would cause his brain to screech to a halt, and he could think of nothing else.

All of this was disconcerting to Jack. He loved his wife. But he couldn't remember the last time he felt as exhilarated with her as he did with . . . *her.*

In the book *Lucky in Love,* Catherine Johnson points out that infatuation, or falling in love, is like a powerful drug. It takes over your life. It is a wonderful feeling. But like any drug effect, it wears off. And you require higher doses of it to get the same effect that a lower dose gave you before. Married couples get used to one another. They can still arouse and titillate, and certainly can excite each other with their passion. And the happiest of couples—no matter how long they've been married—will report that they still get sexually charged when with their mate. But the effect is usually weaker than it was years ago, or not as long-lasting, and they may require more of a jump-start to get the machinery working. That is why novelty—going on vacation, or making love in a room other than a bedroom—is useful for couples who've been together a long time. In fact, Catherine Johnson suggests that periods of sexual disengagement are sometimes necessary to spark intense and renewed sexual involvement.

So what was Jack's problem? He yearned for the exhilarating feeling that had recently resurfaced in him. He wondered whether perhaps the absence of that feeling when he was with his wife implied a problem in the marriage. He didn't want an affair. He certainly didn't want to lose his marriage. But . . . . Well, does one have to give up that great feeling altogether?

Jack had a busy life. Too may work hours, too few leisure hours. His wife was very busy too. When he thought of her he thought of his responsibilities. When he thought of the woman down the hall, he thought of freedom from responsibilities. He thought of a future of pleasure and contentment, a casting-off of the shackles of everyday life. A woman who'd understand—really understand him.

"What do you do that gets in the way of your wife's understanding you?" I asked.

The question surprised him. I wanted him to realize that his actions influenced his wife's actions (and vice versa).

"I guess I don't talk to her much. Not about me anyway. I talk about bills and the kids. I don't talk about my dreams or fantasies."

"But you fantasize discussing those things with the other woman, and that makes her more appealing."

"Yes. I guess you're suggesting that if I talked more with my wife about my dreams, I'd be more attracted to her."

I nodded.

"Jack, imagine that a man who works down the hall from your wife is very infatuated with her. What does he see in her that you don't?"

"It makes me uncomfortable just thinking about that possibility," Jack said. "I guess he'd like her body. She's still in pretty good shape. But I think he'd be attracted to her lust for life. She can get so happy and excited over mundane things. My favorite times with her were in the autumn. She'd wear this flannel shirt that somehow made her eyes shine. And we'd take long walks, or hike up a mountain trail. She loved nature. She really excited me then."

Jack had a smile on his face.

"That part of her personality is still there, Jack. It probably just got submerged under the diapers and bills and grass clippings you two have accumulated over the years."

Jack went home that day and scoured his wife's closet for her old flannel shirt. He found it, went to her in the kitchen, and asked whether she would wear it, because he always thought she looked so sexy in it. He helped her remove her blouse . . .

Jack called me a few days later to say his old feelings of passion for his wife had reemerged.

When Sex Isn't Simple

Sexual problems can occur at any point along the *sexual response cycle*. The first stage of the cycle is *desire*. The most common complaint at this phase is low or inadequate desire. The second phase is *arousal*. Common problems here are difficulty becoming aroused or maintaining a state of arousal. Impotence is a disorder of arousal. The third stage is *orgasm*. Premature orgasm, delayed orgasm, or inability to reach orgasm are problems at that stage.

A fourth kind of difficulty—which may involve problems already cited—is mismatched desire. Here, couples can't get in sync with one another sexually. Or, one person wants to have sex more frequently than his or her partner does.

Of these four problems, the most frequent are lack of desire and mismatched desire. For many couples, the presence of one of these problems may be annoying but poses no threat to the stability of the relationship. In fact, a *New England Journal of Medicine* study of one hundred educated couples (average age was thirty-three) revealed that one-half of the men and over three-fourths of the women reported a periodic lack of interest in sex. Nonetheless, 85 percent of the respondents reported a satisfying sex life overall, despite any current complaints. Of these "normal" people, 40 percent of the men reported occasional erectile or ejaculatory problems, while 63 percent of the women reported problems with arousal or orgasm. Lovemaking occurred once a week, on average.

So sexual difficulties and let downs are not uncommon; nor need they always be a problem for a couple. But for many, sexual concerns don't fade over time. If sexual problems persist, or if feelings of anger, guilt, or anxiety replace passion and romance, steps must be taken to resolve matters.

Problems of Desire

If you had a bad cold, the flu, or a toothache, sex would not interest you. That makes sense, but still many people overlook the fact that lifestyles—hectic work schedules, home responsibilities, deadlines—can interfere with one's capacity to enjoy sex. Many folks are too tired at the end of the day to think about sex and have no time during the middle of the day to engage in it. Many nonsexual reasons exist for so-called sexual problems. (See "Marriage Matters".)

MARRIAGE MATTERS

If a sexual problem persists, or if the presence of any sexual difficulty worries you, first consider what nonsexual factors may be accounting for your trouble. Dr. Frank Bruno, in his book *Psychological Symptoms*, offers the following guidelines:

- Physical or biological problems can cause sexual problems. For example, a man with atherosclerosis (blocked arteries) may not be able to get or maintain an erection, as the penile arteries are also blocked. Diabetes can cause arousal problems for men too, and low levels of hormones in the blood can reduce sexual desire or excitement for men and women.

- Medication side effects may account for sexual difficulties. For instance, high blood pressure medication and antidepressant medication may diminish sexual functioning.

- Moderate and regular exercise can stimulate endorphin production in the brain, which can improve your mood and responsiveness to sexual stimuli.

- Alcohol can get you in the mood if it releases your inhibitions, but too much alcohol will diminish your capacity to stay aroused.

- Concerns about physical appearance (facial blemishes or sores) or unhappiness with one's physique can cause a person to lose interest in sex.

♥ ♥ ♥

In his book *A Lifelong Love Affair,* Joseph Nowinski reported that low sexual desire can sometimes be a simple consequence of careless grooming and style of dress. Some people pay little attention to how their hair looks or whether their clothes are too tight or too loose. A comfortable weekend outfit may be a turn off to a mate if the outfit is shabby. Nowinski cited examples of people who made themselves look better and consequently felt better about themselves. Their improved attitude gave a needed boost to their sex life, as well. New hair styles (not just for women), a new set of comfortable but attractive clothes, a commitment to eating right and exercising, can all add zest to your sex appeal and make you feel better about yourself.

Kate didn't like her appearance. She was fifty pounds overweight. Even breathing was sometimes difficult, let alone sex. But after losing her first six pounds, her mood improved and so did her sexual appetite. She was still more than forty pounds overweight, but her initial progress in weight reduction was enough to spark her old passions.

♥ ♥ ♥

RED FLAGS

Sexual concerns will be more likely to occur if any of the following factors are present:

- History of physical abuse, sexual abuse, or rape
- Persistent stress in daily life
- Negative attitudes about sexuality when you were a child
- Lack of physical affection when growing up
- Persistent dissatisfaction with your mate
- Inability to discuss sexual matters with your mate
- Recent job loss or blow to your self-esteem

♥ ♥ ♥

Problems of sexual desire also occur when a couple simply aren't getting along in other areas of their marriage.

Resentments, misunderstandings, little time to spend together, disagreements about finances or the children—all can interfere with sexual desire and responsiveness. When a couple have been distant emotionally from one another, sex means something different to each of the spouses.

To men, making love is often their way of feeling loved. Women do not usually need to make love to feel loved.

Consequently, men sometimes seem to be pushing for sex with little thought for affection and holding, because they want to feel loved. But women sometimes withhold sex because they need affection and holding to feel loved.

Women sometimes say "no" to sex as a way to invite closeness.

Men push for sex as a way to invite closeness. Without a basic understanding of that fundamental difference between the sexes, spouses will misperceive their partner's motives and feel resentful.

Finally, sexual desire problems occur when one or both partners hold dear to mistaken beliefs about sex and sexual performance. Common misbeliefs:

- It is essential to satisfy your partner every time

- Reaching orgasm is vital for sexual satisfaction
- Sexual fantasies are wrong
- If you want sex often, you are exploiting your partner
- A sexually aggressive woman is a turn-off to her mate
- A desire for sexual experimentation is a sign of perversion
- If sexual desire is on the wane, it is an indication you have fallen out of love

A more realistic view of the above sentiments is as follows:

- "Satisfaction" is obtained when spouses are tender, considerate, and desirous of making love. Thinking you need to bring your partner to heights of sexual ecstasy every time you make love is unrealistic (and unnecessary for sexual fulfillment), and will lead to performance anxiety.

- Orgasm is not essential for sexual satisfaction. Many couples will from time to time forego orgasm in lovemaking so as to enhance other aspects of sexual relating. Women, on average, reach orgasm about 50 percent of the time they make love. Men much more than women believe orgasm is essential, probably because men achieve orgasm nearly all the time they make love.

- Sexual fantasies are forever. They are not helpful if a spouse avoids sex with a partner so as to fantasize about someone else. For happy couples, sexual fantasies (from watching a movie or reading a book) often spark their desire and passion for one another.

- You are exploiting your partner only if you ignore his or her wishes and desires. It is rare for a couple to be in perfect sync with each other sexually. Commonly, one spouse can get by with less sex than the other.

- In study after study, the number-one sexual complaint men have about their partners is *passivity*. So a sexually aggressive woman is *not* a turn-off to her mate.

- Imaginative sex play often adds zest to one's love life. In one study, women over forty who engaged in acts of "sexual abandon" with their mates reported feeling more special and worthwhile.

- Sexual desire can lessen for many reasons: stress, health problems, medication side-effects, hormonal fluctuations, and unrealistic or irrational beliefs about sexual functioning. Remember, "normal" and "satisfied" couples will report diminished sexual desire on occasion.

Any irrational beliefs you hold about sexuality can threaten your satisfaction with your relationship. Our brains function to protect us from threatening situations by signaling the glands to release chemicals, (such as adrenaline) in the bloodstream, to help us fight or flee—to prevent us from becoming sexually aroused. (The human animal would have become extinct eons ago if it got horny every time it was threatened.) In other words, anxiety overrules sexual arousal. You will have sexual difficulties when anxiety accompanies you to the bedroom.

The most typical (and unhelpful) thing people who have anxiety about their sexual performance do is *tune in to signs of anxiety or inadequate sexual responsiveness while they are attempting to make love.* They become a "spectator" to their own performance, which has the effect of reducing their arousal and performance capability. So the man with arousal difficulties distracts himself from the sexual act when he notices his penis is no longer as hard, becomes anxious about that (which makes him lose his erection entirely), and feels like a failure. Pleasurable and fulfilling lovemaking requires one to concentrate on what's right, not on what's wrong. "Sensate Focus" is a most useful technique for couples who wish to improve sexual desire and reduce performance anxiety. See "Building a Successful Relationship."

♥ ♥ ♥

BUILDING A SUCCESSFUL RELATIONSHIP

The "Sensate Focus" technique is especially helpful when one or both spouses has experienced excessive anxiety about the ability to maintain sexual arousal. The technique is also helpful for couples whose sex life has become mundane.

The ultimate goal is to eliminate anxiety and enhance sexual pleasure. The immediate goal is to learn to enjoy each other physically but not sexually. When the pressure to perform is off and expectations are low, couples often learn to enjoy simple physical pleasures they've ignored.

First the couple take turns stroking and caressing each other (clothed or unclothed) with no touching of the breasts or genitals. The entire time should be spent doing that. No sexual touching of any kind is allowed. This activity may continue the next time the couple is together, or they may proceed to the next step.

Next, couples are allowed to touch the breasts or genitals while stroking the rest of the body. While sexual arousal may or may not occur, arousal is not the aim. The goal is to learn to be comfortable touching one another in a sexual area without expecting sexual arousal.

At a different time, the couple may progress to genital stimulation, in addition to general body caressing. However, orgasm is not to be attempted or achieved. Again, there is no emphasis on performance. Since intercourse and orgasm are not allowed, arousal may wax and wane without disappointment.

Finally, when each partner is willing, they may allow themselves to move from caressing to genital touching to genital stimulation and finally to orgasm.

♥ ♥ ♥

Getting to the Heart of the Matter

Like any other area of conflict or consternation, sexual problems need not persist. But often they do. Three reasons predominate:

1. Even couples who communicate effectively are reluctant to discuss their sexual relationship or concerns. Consequently, "ignorance" perpetuates the problem.

2. One's sex appeal and expertise in lovemaking are often significant aspects to one's self-esteem. One common method people use to protect their self-esteem is to blame someone else for their difficulties rather than honestly appraise their own role in a problem. Consequently, partner with sexual problems may be quick to blame one another.

3. Couples often reapply failed solutions to a sex problem. For example, avoidance of sex reduces anxiety about performance in the short run but does nothing to alleviate the anxiety over time. Thus, when a "sex avoider" finally gives in and attempts to make love, his or her anxiety will reduce both pleasure and performance, resulting in more avoidance of sex.

Elliot complained that Liz was rarely interested in having sex. "And when we do, her heart isn't in it. Mostly she tells me she's too tired and that I should understand that. I don't understand."

"Part of the problem," said Liz, "is that Elliot wants to 'have sex.' He's not interested in making love."

" 'Having sex' is just a phrase. You know what I mean by it."

"I'm not sure what you mean. You rarely want to spend time with me anymore. You're not romantic. You always discount my feelings when I want to talk about our relationship. Why should I want to go to bed with you?"

"Now that's the real problem," Elliot said, turning to me. "Did you hear what she said? She said I'm not romantic and I don't care about her feelings. Do you know how often she criticizes me? Even over little things—a coffee cup left on the table overnight, questioning my judgment on a route we take when we're driving somewhere. I try to shrug those complaints off.

"Isn't that the mature thing to do? And when I want to make love more than once a month she finds excuses not to, and tells me I'm responsible for her bad attitude."

"I don't always criticize you, Elliot. I can't offer a suggestion or an opinion without you thinking I'm finding fault. Your self-esteem is poor. That's *your* problem."

Applying the Formula

Step One: Unhooking Emotional Triangles

Liz and Elliot were not unique. It is too much to expect any couple to be in perfect sync with each other sexually. Satisfied couples don't take it personally when their mate says, "Not tonight." And often they are willing to try to "get in the mood" when they are not in the mood. A little give and take and a dollop of understanding go a long way to help smooth over the wrinkles in a sexual relationship.

There were no key triangles for Liz and Elliot. True, on occasion one of them would cite the children or job stress as a reason not to make love, but that wasn't always the case. Their biggest issue was that they each felt poorly treated and misunderstood by the other. Improving the way they got along overall seemed to be essential to improving their sexual relationship.

Step Two: Examining Your Role in the Problem

Liz and Elliot each acted in self-defeating ways without being aware of it.

1. Each reapplied failed solutions. To Liz, the "solution" to Elliot's tendency to ignore her or be unaffectionate was to withhold sex. But that only made Elliot more upset and increased the odds that the next time they were sexual he'd head straight for the meat and potatoes and forget the appetizer.

   She also criticized him occasionally. Like many men, Elliot took criticisms—even small ones—to heart. And he did not forget them. Consequently he was less likely to be interested in her feelings and opinions, viewing her as judgmental.

   To Elliot, the "solution" to reengage Liz in sex was to wait patiently until he believed she had had enough celibacy for one week, then pounce. He felt that by holding off awhile he was respecting her wishes, and therefore had a right to expect her to comply with his wish for sex, when he finally asked. He'd complain when she'd say "no," sulk for a week (ignoring her in the process), and then resume panting, feeling even more entitled to sex. It didn't work the first time he did it, and it didn't work the tenth time he did it. But he kept doing it.

   Elliot also refused to see the merit to Liz's complaints. He *wasn't* romantic—at least not as he once had been. But he focused on her complaint about it as being the problem. His "solution" to get her to stop criticizing was to stubbornly resist being romantic. His attitude was, "You think I'm unromantic? I'll show you what unromantic *really* is." His "solution" made the problem worse.

2. Liz believed she could view their problem with pristine clarity. Elliot, for the most part, was the problem. Whenever she did things he objected to, it was because she had "good reason." Whenever Elliot did things she objected to, it was because he didn't care.

Deep down, Elliot believed Liz was primarily to blame. Perhaps he wasn't as romantic as he might be, but it's hard to feel playful with someone who rejects your advances. He had "good reason" to do what he did. Her reasons were not good enough.

It took a while for Liz and Elliot to own, the fact that they each acted in counterproductive ways and used a double standard when evaluating behavior. Liz admitted it wasn't fair to judge Elliot as uncaring or selfish when he acted in a manner she disliked—if she wasn't willing to judge her own behavior by the same standards. Elliot agreed that he had been unfair, too.

Both agreed to stop applying solutions that only made their problem worse. Elliot agreed to show more affection and not expect that affection must always lead to sex. Liz agreed not to withhold sex as a punishment. If she was upset with Elliot, she'd talk about her concerns instead.

For the time being (at least thirty days), it was decided that Liz alone would be the sexual initiator. They had been stuck in a pursuer-distancer pattern for too long, with Elliot as the sexual pursuer and Liz as the sexual distancer. Elliot needed to believe that Liz could respond sexually without always needing to be prodded, and Liz needed to see that Elliot could spend time with her in nonsexual ways.

Step Three: Uncovering Hidden Agendas

Liz's underlying concern had to do with *interest*. Was Elliot really *interest*ed in her for reasons other than sex? Her complaints about his sexual advances were really complaints about his lack of interest in her. He rarely spoke to her except about superficial matters. He preferred watching television to going out together. Was he truly attracted to her anymore? Or was sex just fulfilling a biological need for Elliot?

As is typical for couples with hidden agendas, the hidden concern rarely gets discussed, except indirectly. They argue about sex or time together, but they don't discuss the heart of the matter.

There were two hidden agendas for Elliot. First, he too was troubled by Liz's apparent lack of interest in him. He pursued her for sex—perhaps more than he ordinarily would—because he needed reassurance from her that she was still interested in him. When she turned him down, his fears of not being desirable increased, prompting him periodically to push for more sex. He worked hard, usually fifty hours a week. Didn't she realize that watching television was his way of unwinding? Wasn't he entitled to that?

He also had an issue of *fairness,* or *control.* She called the shots, sexually speaking, and it wasn't fair. Even if she grudgingly agreed to have sex, she "won," because he wasn't really interested in having sex with her unless she was eager. She'd withhold sex, so he'd withhold affection. His "two can play at this game" mentality revealed his underlying issue about lack of fairness.

Given these concerns, the couple agreed to do the following:

- Elliot agreed to show more of an interest in Liz. He had been not only the sexual pursuer but the "emotional distancer." (Liz was the sexual distancer and emotional pursuer.) Showing greater emotional interest in Liz was essential for their mutual satisfaction, just as Liz's willingness to pursue him sexually was important.

- Liz agreed not to criticize Elliot automatically for watching television. If she wanted time with him, she'd tell him so. But she'd also let him know she understood that he might need time to himself to unwind.

Step Four: Examining Your Past

Liz was the youngest in a family of five. Although not pampered, she was accustomed to a great deal of attention from people without having to do anything other than "be there to receive it." She realized that her childhood had a lot to do with the distress she experienced when Elliot seemed to ignore her (except for sex).

Elliot had younger siblings and one older sister. He remembered having considerable authority and responsibility growing up, "being the eldest boy," but he also recalled having to submit to his older sister's rule on occasion.

"I never felt fully appreciated by my family for all I had to do. To add insult to injury, I'd sometimes be expected to go along with my older sister's dictates, even though I thought she was wrong."

For Elliot, Liz was his older sister all over again. She criticized him—the way his sister did—and had ultimate control. Elliot sometimes resisted his sister's expectations of him just because he was angry and wanted to "show her she couldn't control me." This was remarkably similar to the way in which he often responded to Liz's requests.

I reminded Liz and Elliot that it was no accident they had chosen one another as mates. Probably what annoyed each of them about the other had to do with areas of their own personality that needed some fixing. Liz needed to feel good about herself without always needing to be being fussed over by Elliot, and Elliot needed to cooperate with Liz without feeling controlled.

They also agreed to alter their way of relating to their siblings. Liz wanted to spend time with them without always acting like the "youngest one in the family," and Elliot wanted to be with his family without acting like the boss.

Keep in Mind

- Novelty and imaginative sex play are important. They can rejuvenate your sexual attraction to your mate.

- Diminished sexual desire is a common complaint, even among happy couples. Desire can lessen as a result of stress, hormonal imbalances, medication side-effects, and marital misunderstandings.

- Many men who "know" they are loved still need to make love to "feel" loved. Men who complain they aren't getting enough sex are often complaining they don't get enough love.

- Many women who "know" they are loved need tenderness and affection to "feel" loved. Women who complain they aren't getting enough affection are often complaining they aren't getting enough love.

- The number-one sexual complaint men have about women: being too passive in bed.

- The number-one complaint women have about men: being too genitally focused.

Chapter 14

When Balancing Career and Family Is the Problem

"I quit my job. I wasn't all that happy at work and our home life suffered. Meals were stressful, evenings were chaotic. Money is tight now that I'm home, but everyone seems to get along better." Janice, age 33.

"I'm a happier person now that I'm working. I feel challenged by what I do. Home life is more hectic, but we are all adjusting fine. Actually, I'm a more attentive mother and wife now that I'm working." Marge, age 38.

"The best word to describe how I feel is 'Aargh.' I know my job stress affects my family life and I hate that. But I make a good living and that must count for something. Right?" John, age 41.

Today's dual-career couples are the pioneers (or the guinea pigs) for the next generation. American society has had to adjust and readjust in an effort to meet the changing needs of families in which the women works. "If it weren't for day care, microwave ovens, Pizza Hut, and Nickelodeon, my family wouldn't function," said one working mother.

The fastest-growing segment of the American work force is mothers with pre-school children. About 60 percent of young mothers are currently employed, and although working mothers have become commonplace, many women still feel guilty about not spending enough time with their children. Many men are having to adopt a more active role in their family as a result of these changes—a good thing but a difficult one, since most men's fathers were the traditional bread winners whose main fathering function was to protect and provide for the family.

Although many new couples desire to play nontraditional roles, there is a tendency for roles to shift back in the direction of tradition once children arrive on the scene. Faced with the sobering responsibilities of parenthood, dads worry about finances (causing them to place work at the center of their lives) and moms worry about raising a family (causing them to place relationships at the center of their lives).

Achieving satisfaction at home and on the job is no easy task, but it is important. Studies indicate that the happiest and healthiest people are active and very satisfied with their jobs *and* their family lives. According to Dr. Blair Justice in his book *Who Gets Sick,* people dissatisfied either at home or on the job tend to smoke and drink more, experience more stress, and develop more illnesses.

Finding the right balance of home and job satisfaction is difficult, primarily because in order to have more satisfaction in one area, you frequently have to sacrifice aspects of the other. Too often people are faced with a choice—either a career with potential for advancement or a family life with parents who are available to the children. Advancing one's career often means putting the family on the back burner. Devotion to family often means standing still on one rung of the career ladder. As one man put it, "I finally got the promotion I deserved, but it meant more travel and time away from home. It was a honey of a job. But it made my home life sticky."

Balancing Career and Family: Where It Gets Sticky

Jobs sometimes interfere with home life, and home life sometimes interferes with job performance. In one study, 56 percent of employed women reported moderate to severe "spillover." With high job strain, family life was adversely affected. With high marital strain, job performance was affected. Women who reported the spillover traveling in both directions also reported feeling depressed or anxious during the previous year.

♥ ♥ ♥

RED FLAGS

If any of the following conditions apply, you are at increased risk for developing conflict—within yourself or between yourself and your mate—over your work and family roles.

- Dual-career couple who work different shifts
- Dual-career couple with small children
- Routine sacrifice of sleep or lunch hours to home chores or child care
- Perception that home chores and child-care responsibilities are unfairly distributed between you and your mate
- A belief that your job and home responsibilities interfere with one another to a large extent
- A tendency to try to get as much work (home and office) accomplished as possible, combined with reluctance to put some chores lower down on the priority list.
- You are working outside the home but really wish you could stay at home

♥ ♥ ♥

Broadly, there are three factors that make coping with career and family more difficult.

Employer Nonsupport for Workers with Children

Slowly but surely American employers are becoming sensitive to the needs of working parents. Many major corporations now allow their workers to arrive for and leave work at hours that are flexible and accommodate children's school hours. Maternity leave for women is common. Paternity leave is allowed in some companies, but many men are uncomfortable with that opportunity, believing it may slow down their career advancement. Nina Youngstrom, reporting in the *APA Monitor,* cites research that concludes parental satisfaction is greatest for working couples whose employers support the needs of families. *Parenting was more difficult the tougher the job, the younger the child, and the less support received from one's boss.*

Inadequate Time for Spouses to Spend with Each Other

In a survey of 2,399 employees of a large corporation, Nina Youngstrom found that 57 percent of respondents saw their jobs as a *serious obstacle* to spending time with their partner. One-third of respondents said they were not in a good mood when they came home from work, and 46 percent said they felt they had to make a choice—job or family.

When it came to making room for jobs, children, chores, and spouses, spouses were most likely to be put aside. (There is evidence that many people feel it is more difficult to find a satisfying job than it is to find a satisfying mate.) Working women are on the job ten more hours per week more than they were in the early 1980s. All of that time spent working comes at the expense of leisure time with their spouse.

In one-quarter of all two-income homes, spouses work different shifts. Those couples complain of poorer health, less sleep, fewer friends, and less leisure time together. Their rate of divorce is slightly higher than the national average.

Gender-role conflict

Men are doing more household chores, but it's the women who are seeing to it that the chores get done. In other words, considerate husbands sometimes view their household chore responsibility as an "assignment" or as "helping out"—an attitude that implies that home care is still primarily a woman's responsibility.

Further, in dual-career households where both parents participate in child-care, it appears that the women are still more likely than the men to take time off from work to accommodate a sick child. Working mothers, more than fathers, get up in the middle of the night with a sick child and leave work early to take the children for routine visits to the doctor or dentist.

And yet in a study by Monica Biernat and Camille Wortman, mothers with professional careers were quite pleased with their husbands' role in child rearing, even though the men were documented to be doing less than the women, but were displeased with their own performance. "I'm not doing enough for my children" was the concern of those mothers. (One reason men do less housework and child care is that their wives feel responsible to do more. If women are willing to do more, many men are happy to let them. Many wives prefer to do some of the chores themselves because they think their husbands are careless and make more mistakes. Probably true. Yet many men resent any criticism to that effect, leading them to do less work around the house.)

In that study, work-home upsets occurred mostly in the morning and late afternoon. In the morning, mothers had to rush to take care of the children's needs before they themselves had to rush to get to work. Late afternoons brought another round of stress for mothers, who had to leave work promptly (or early) to care for children coming home from school. The main coping strategy for many of these women was to "work as hard and efficiently as possible to get everything done." They were disinclined to tell themselves that it was okay not to get everything accomplished. These "Superwomen" were also less likely to divest themselves of some responsibilities. Superwomen also had a tendency to cut back on lunch hours, leisure time, and sleep in order to get more work accomplished.

One might think that in the 1990s attitudes toward working women would be favorable, at least among the next generation. Yet a 1991 study showed that when college students had to evaluate fictitious women based on limited data (married or divorced, mothers, employed or unemployed) the results were unambiguous: Working women were regarded as "competent," but working mothers were rated as less nurturing, less dedicated to the family, and more selfish than their non-working counterparts.

Men still struggle with role conflicts as well. According to Robert Weiss in his book *Staying the Course: The Emotional and Social Lives of Men Who Do Well at Work,* men are often unwilling to discuss work stress with their wives if the stress is due to "unmet challenges." (Unmet challenges usually mean a loss of self-esteem.) Instead men may complain of weariness, because that suggests how hard they are sacrificing for the family. Wives are often aware that their husbands are distressed by their jobs and feel shut out by their husbands' silence. Confronting their husbands with "Is something troubling you about your job?" is likely to be met with "No" or a vague "Just the usual stuff."

Finally, it is often hard for a man (a woman, too) to come home from work and have to fend for himself—make his own dinner or the children's dinner, or assist with dinnertime and after-dinner chores (clean up, bathtime for kids, etc.). In the good old days men were pampered a bit when they arrived home. They were appreciated for their hard work. And the family dinner hour was a fairly reliable ritual. "Family dinner hour?" said one man. "In our house we all eat at different times, depending upon work schedules and the kids' after-school activities. It isn't a *family* activity. And I wouldn't call what we eat *dinner.* Often it's pizza or take-out, a quick bite and we're off doing something else. And no dinner has ever taken an hour. Not even Thanksgiving dinner. The only time we have a family dinner hour is when we all go out to a restaurant, and we have to wait fifty minutes to be served. Does that count?"

Easing the Burden

Dual-career couples with young children have too much to do. Period. One might advise them to hunker down and wait eight or nine years for the little ones to be older, but that is about how long the average marriage lasts. Generally, couples who best manage career and home conflicts do the following:

1. *They don't lose sight of the marriage.* The marriage is the keystone of the family. By keeping their relationship a priority, the family can withstand daily hassles and occasional periods of overinvolvement with one's job.

2. *They say "no" to low-priority tasks and activities.* Successful couples don't try to do everything. The "Superwoman" and "Superman" approach leads to burnout. Setting priorities also adds to the perception of having more *control,* a factor shown to improve stress resilience substantially.

3. *They talk about their stress.* One study revealed that couples under high stress who adopted the values and expectations of the "masculine role" were more dissatisfied with their lives. The components of the masculine role most associated with physical and emotional distress were:

   • *restricted emotionality*—not expressing feelings
   • *reduced affection*—less shows of tenderness and affection
   • *preoccupation with success*—focus on career advancement while neglecting relationships

   Taking time to talk about stressful life events with a mate provides relief and builds intimacy.

4. *They don't try to work and engage in family activities at the same time.* Busy parents often try to play with the kids *and* concentrate on a business presentation all at once, thereby doing neither very well.

   "If I'm with the family, I must learn to be fully with them," one harried father explained. "Too often I'd interrupt family activities to make business phone calls. As much as possible I want to be fully present when I'm with my wife and children, not a preoccupied bystander."

5. They are involved in at least one regular family ritual. Going to church every week, having a regular weekend outing, bedtime stories—all of those contribute to a sense of predictability in an otherwise fast-paced family week. Successful families convey a sense of *wanting* to spend time together, then they do it.

Prioritizing, making the marriage the centerpiece of the family, self-disclosure, shows of affection, and family rituals can all be a part of your life. By taking the reins of control over life events instead of being dragged along by them, you can improve your resilience to stress. Research shows that people who believe they have more say-so over events affecting their life are healthier, happier, and likely to live longer.

♥ ♥ ♥

MARRIAGE MATTERS

When women work, who fares better? Husbands or wives?

According to research evidence, wives fare better. While work can be drudgery for many people, overall a wife who works and who wants to work is very happy with her situation. The next-happiest wife is the one who is unemployed and wishes to be unemployed. The least-happy wife is one who wants to work but cannot.[1]

On the other hand, a careful analysis of data from a number of studies reveals that husbands exhibit increased distress when their wives work. Overall, such men are at higher risk for feeling depressed or experiencing a decline in self-esteem. There is no evidence that such consequences are due to men's increased responsibilities at home when their wives are working. The distress is greatest for men between the ages of thirty-five and fifty. Evidently, men in that age group require more support from their wives, which is usually less available when the women are working.[2]

♥ ♥ ♥

Getting to the Heart of the Matter

As an insurance salesman, Neil was required to schedule many evening appointments. Lynn was accustomed to his schedule until the birth of their second child; then the all-consuming chores of parenthood, combined with the fact that Lynn held a day job, made Neil's evening absences tiresome. She understood what Neil's job required him to do, but she didn't like it. Most frustrating for her, however, was Neil's tendency to miscalculate his hours. "I'll be home by eight-thirty," he might say, and then he'd arrive home at a quarter to ten.

"I can't predict how many questions a new client might ask me," Neil argued in his defense. "Some appointments run longer than others. You should know that by now, Lynn."

"I do understand," answered Lynn. "But virtually every night you come home much later than you said you would. I get the feeling you don't try very hard to get home as soon as possible."

Neil sighed. And he thought of his almost daily preoccupation with making sure he isn't late for his appointments so that Lynn wouldn't be upset with him. He thought of the client he put off for a week just so he could get home early one night. And he wondered why he tried so hard to come home early when he got no credit for it. What he got instead was the baby and a bottle and a "Take him, he's yours" from Lynn.

"How long has this been going on?" I asked.

"About two years," Neil answered. "I'm trying to build my business. I can't very well turn down customers just yet, especially with a new baby. More than ever I worry that I'm not earning enough money. But I don't think Lynn realizes how bogged down I am with my responsibilities to her, the kids, and my employer."

Neil was typical. A family man at heart, the arrival of children sparked an instinctive drive to "protect" and "provide" for the family. He didn't tell Lynn just how much he worried about money. He wanted to protect her from his concerns. He had also felt some chest pains while exercising last week. That worried him too, but it was better not tell Lynn.

"I think you're overworked," Neil said to Lynn. "I've told you before to cut back your work hours. We can still get by."

"That's another problem, Neil. I'm not sure you respect what I do for a living. Why don't you cut back on your hours?"

"I have a territory to cover. If I cut back hours and don't cover the territory, they'll give it to somebody else. I'll never make my way successfully in this business if I do that." Not only were they unable to come to some satisfying solution to this longstanding problem, their expectation was that things wouldn't improve while Neil was still building up a clientele.

Applying the Formula

Step One: Unhooking Emotional Triangles

At first glance it seemed that a workplace triangle was operating, since Neil and Lynn argued about his work hours. But upon further examination it became clear that Neil didn't work longer hours as a way to avoid dealing with Lynn. So no emotional triangle was evident from that perspective. However, Lynn admitted that on evenings when she and Neil might be able to spend some romantic time together, she would insist she needed that time for herself. While time for individual pursuits or relaxation is important, it was clear that Lynn avoided being alone with Neil. When confronted, she explained that she was overtired because of the effort she regularly put forth to accommodate his work schedule. In fact then, a work triangle did exist. Lynn focused on the issue of Neil's job precisely when the two of them could have spent enjoyable time together.

Neil understood this to mean that Lynn still resented his overtime hours. And he realized that they'd grown more distant since the birth of their second child.

They agreed to spend some romantic time together once a week. Neil took responsibility for making babysitter arrangements. And Lynn agreed to act more warmly on some evenings when Neil arrived home late. She had a right to be frustrated by his work hours, but she didn't want to add to the negativity by only showing frustration and resentment.

BUILDING A SUCCESSFUL RELATIONSHIP

Couples in conflict often spend less and less time together, living separately under one roof. Improving companionship activities is important to building intimacy and reestablishing warmth. But it is not easy to do. Although spending less time together will diminish marital satisfaction, automatically spending more time together may be "too much too soon" for couples who haven't worked out some of the kinks in their relationship. It's best to start small and work your way up. These guidelines can help:

- If you're planning to go on a date together, plan in advance. Who will make the reservations? What night will you go out? Who will arrange for a babysitter? Do you have a back-up plan?

- A getaway vacation is nice. But start with an overnight at a hotel or a brief two-day vacation. Better to return wishing you could have stayed longer than to stay too long and argue.

- Expect to feel a bit awkward if you're not accustomed to spending so much time together. You will feel self-conscious; so will your mate. Don't worry about it.

- On any outing together, anticipate what could happen that would be an obstacle to enjoying the time together. Then plan a strategy to handle the situation should it arise.

♥ ♥ ♥

Step Two: Examining Your Role in the Problem

The first thing examined was whether Neil or Lynn was reapplying a "solution" that only made matters worse.

"Neil," I said, "one of Lynn's pet peeves is that you promise her you'll be home at one time, yet you often arrive home much later . . ."

". . . But I can't always predict how long my appointments will last," Neil said, interrupting.

"We know that. But then why not tell Lynn you'll be home later than you think? That way you'll often be on time, or even a little early."

"I've thought of that," Neil answered, "but I didn't want to see the look on Lynn's face when I tell her I'll be home late. Besides, I keep telling myself that with discipline I can get home on time. I don't want to get home any later than I have to."

"So it sounds to me that in order to help Lynn feel better, you'd set an unrealistic appointment schedule—with every good intention of trying to meet it."

"That's right," said Neil.

"But because it was unrealistic, your appointments run overtime, you arrive home late, and Lynn is angry because you promised her you'd be home early that night."

"Right again," said Neil.

"And because she's angry, you promise you'll absolutely be home early from now on—which is unrealistic in your business. It's a vicious cycle."

Neil agreed that the only sensible thing to do was to set up fewer appointments, or tell Lynn he'd be coming home an hour or so later than he thinks is realistic.

"It would help me a lot to be able to count on you coming home when you say you will. I think I could tolerate your hours better if you weren't so unpredictable. It's no fun planning dinner only to have it grow cold, or planning on taking a shower when you get home only to have to wait an extra sixty minutes."

Neil also agreed that for a while he would eliminate one late evening appointment every two weeks from his schedule, insuring he'd be home earlier that evening. It was a sacrifice he was willing to make.

Lynn realized that her constant complaining about Neil's hours hadn't helped him to be more timely. In fact, it only raised his anxiety and prompted him to make promises he couldn't realistically keep—which made her complain even more. She agreed to complain less and find more positive things to say to him when he arrived home.

Step Three: Uncovering Hidden Agendas

Lynn worried that Neil was a bit too controlling. He might discuss matters with her, but usually he got his way. And he seemed unenthusiastic about her working. He acted like he wanted her to quit, though he never actually said that. Feeling a bit one-down with Neil, Lynn tried to make the relationship more equitable by insisting he immediately care for the baby when he came home at night.

But that only fueled Neil's hidden fear that Lynn no longer cared about him as much as she once did. Didn't she understand how hard he worked? Couldn't she figure out that he'd much rather be home every night than out working, but that he really had little choice?

By putting these concerns on the table, the couple could make rapid progress in overcoming their problem. Lynn needed to feel like Neil's equal in the marriage. Neil needed to feel cared about. Lynn asked Neil to find something positive to say about her job instead of subtly criticizing it. She wanted him to ask her more about how her day at the office went rather than ignore the topic. He agreed. Neil asked Lynn to give him a warm welcome-home kiss at night instead of a harsh "It's about time!" comment. She agreed.

Step Four: Examining Your Past

No obviously relevant issue from Lynn's past seemed to be playing a role in the continuation of their problem. Not much from Neil's past seemed relevant either, until he spoke about his father. His dad had been a hard worker who had rarely had time to spend with the family. From about age six, Neil spent less time with his parents. His father was always at work, and his mother—well, Neil preferred the company of his friends.

"I guess it bothered me that my father wasn't around, but I got used to it. It probably toughened me up," he said, smiling.

As a boy, Neil did what many young boys with absent fathers did: He took care of himself and learned to hide his feelings of hurt or loss. Except that now, as an adult, Neil has maintained that stance. Neil does have two children, but he rarely speaks of the older child.

"Luke is seven. I'm sure he's a happy kid. He has lots of friends. I wish I had more time to spend with him."

Neil was beginning to understand that his son had a father who was absent, too. Yes, making a living is important. But was Neil underestimating the importance of his role as father? Probably. Like his own dad, Neil was growing more detached from his family, all in an effort to provide for their welfare.

"My son is learning karate," Neil said. "I think they have father-son lessons. Maybe I should join with him."

"Go for it," I said.

Keep in Mind

- Couples all across America are juggling career and family responsibilities and finding it difficult. You're not alone.

- On average, job stress spills over to one's family life more than family stress spills over to one's job. The higher the stress in one area, the more likely it will be to spill over to the other area.

- Despite enlightened attitudes, working mothers still feel they are not doing enough for their children. In fact, they are probably doing more than their husbands.

- With hours devoted to work and child care, leisure time for couples is at a premium. Take advantage of every moment you and your mate spend together. Like water in a desert, leisure time together for dual-career is their most precious resource.

Chapter 15

When Mistrust Is the Problem

Imagine that each night you enjoy taking a stroll in your neighborhood. You're relaxed, your mind is uncluttered, and you return home refreshed.

Now imagine that a series of frightening crimes have recently occurred in your part of town. So you stay home at night. When you do venture out you are tense and hypervigilant—ready to make a move if you hear or see anything suspicious. Your mind is filled with thoughts of "What if . . .?" You take nothing for granted. And you return home feeling agitated instead of relaxed.

When trust is lost, you can't feel safe. And you can't focus on anything that is good because you're preoccupied with what could be bad.

The same thing happens in a marriage when you've been betrayed or lied to.

Once you can no longer fully trust your mate, everything in the relationship changes. One woman compared the loss of trust in her marriage to a car accident: "The car was badly damaged after the collision. Weeks later I had it back from the repair shop. It looked fine. But it never ran quite the same again."

In order for us to get along in the game of life, we need to know that the other guy is playing fairly and by the rules. A simple act of driving a car is reasonably safe only when other drivers obey the guidelines. Driving in some big cities can be a nerve-wracking experience precisely because many drivers make up their own rules: They cut you off, they run red lights, they veer in and out of traffic without warning. The slogan "watch out for the other guy" is never more valid than in big-city traffic. It means, "Be alert for danger." It's important and necessary to be cautious when danger is possible. But if you must be cautious and alert in your relationship, if you cannot trust fully, your relationship will wear you out and drag you down.

When You Cannot Trust

In a marriage, you're asking about trust when you're asking:

> *Is my spouse reliable?*
> *Is my spouse faithful?*
> *Is my spouse telling me the truth?*

A *reliable* spouse is one you can count on. He's there when he says he'll be there, and he keeps his promises. You can count on him to find work, make a living and not spend money foolishly. He is committed to you. Spouses with addictions—drugs, alcohol, gambling—are notoriously unreliable. They say one thing but frequently do another.

A *faithful* spouse is monogamous. Not only does she not have sexual affairs, she doesn't have "emotional affairs"—emotionally exciting interludes where she bares all of her feelings to another man she feels attracted to. And she is faithful to the commitment you made to one another. She doesn't abandon the relationship at the first sign of problems.

An *honest* spouse doesn't lie, withhold the truth, or beat around the bush. "Full disclosure" is not necessary for a satisfying relationship. Everyone is entitled to privacy. But an honest spouse doesn't keep important secrets from his or her mate.

Whenever any problem or conflict recurs repeatedly, it is a sign that trust has weakened.

Remember, it is not differences of opinion that divide spouses, it is the manner in which those differences get handled. Conflicts don't recur if they get handled properly. If mishandled, they usually lead to hurt feelings, accusations, and defensiveness—all of which lowers your opinion of your partner. He or she is no longer someone you can open up your heart to. All of which kindles mistrust.

Mistrust is as corrosive as acid in a relationship.

1. Mistrust limits intimacy. You simply cannot bare your soul and admit vulnerabilities to a partner who might use what you say against you. With diminished intimacy, you and your mate start to drift away from one another, further weakening any bond of closeness.

2. Mistrust dilutes passion. You cannot be fully sexual if you cannot trust. Mistrust fuels anxiety and vigilance, both of which impede sexual performance. As your sexual relationship weakens, another strand of intimacy breaks within the fabric of your marriage.

3. Mistrust weakens your commitment to your marriage. When you cannot trust, thoughts of separation or divorce recur and provide a feeling of relief.

4. When you cannot trust, you will overlook or minimize any good aspects of your relationship, since you must be on guard for the hurtful aspects. Consequently, the marriage will seem worse than it is.

When intimacy is restricted, when passion is stifled, when commitment is held back, when you can't see the good in the relationship, what's left to hold the relationship together?

RED FLAGS

The more these indicators apply to you or your marriage, the more likely mistrust will be to pose a problem:

- You or your mate has a history of being sexually abused or abandoned at an early age
- You've been betrayed in a previous relationship
- Your partner "flies off the handle"
- You or your mate are "thin-skinned" and quick to feel criticized
- You have a general belief that most people would take advantage of you if they could
- Your mate makes and acts on important decisions but only informs you after the fact
- Commitment to the relationship is weak

♥ ♥ ♥

One woman learned that her husband had had a brief affair three years earlier. The affair was over and the husband wanted his marriage to work. "But I can't help thinking that all the nice things he's done for me over the years were just ways for him to alleviate his guilt. Or maybe he wanted to keep me off his trail. All I know is, I don't know what to believe anymore."

Once you discover that your mate has lied to you about something crucial, or betrayed your trust in some way, your world turns upside down. You question everything you once believed. Doubt haunts you, even over minor events. *Is he really at an office meeting? Why did he hang up the phone the moment I entered the room? Who was he talking to?*

When one spouse feels lied to or betrayed by the other, they often fluctuate from periods of high-intensity involvement to high-intensity detachment. One day they are probing, hunting, spying, clutching. The next day they are cold, aloof, distant. One day it's *Why won't you spend time with me?* the next day it's *Leave me alone.* Chronic mistrust leads to emotional exhaustion.

After the Affair: Rekindling Trust

Unfaithfulness can ruin a marriage. While sexual betrayal is painful, it is usually the deceit surrounding the affair that unravels a marriage.

When an affair is no longer a secret, and both spouses wish somehow to repair their marriage, their efforts to reconcile follow a fairly predictable pattern.

1. The betrayed spouse feels devastated. If that spouse had suspected something was wrong, he or she may experience a sense of relief that "I wasn't crazy to have suspicions." Nonetheless, there is a feeling that one's world

has been upended. It's hard to concentrate on anything but the betrayal. Sleeplessness, angry outbursts, and mood swings develop.

2. Even if there is agreement to work matters out, the betrayed spouse has intense mixed feelings. Some couples report highly passionate lovemaking at this time, followed quickly by venomous anger on the part of the betrayed spouse.

3. The betrayed spouse often becomes preoccupied to the point of obsession with the "facts" of the affair. Questions about who, what, when, where, how, and why—especially why—swirl in his or her mind. Many spouses want to know, in graphic detail, the specifics of what took place sexually between their partner and the other person. They are both repulsed by, yet obsessed with, their need to know everything down to the last detail. *Did you shower together? Did you perform oral sex? When you kissed her, what went through your mind? How often did you have sex? Where did you go to have it?*

    In addition to the sexual details, virtually every betrayed spouse wants to unravel all the lies that were told. *"So when you left the house that Saturday morning to do some shopping, you actually went to meet her. Is that right? And when I asked you if something was wrong and you said you were worried about something at work, you were lying then, weren't you?"* Every lie, every unfaithful encounter, must be examined and reexamined.

4. At this point, the unfaithful spouse is confused, worried, and unsure how best to respond to his or her mate. On the one hand, he wants the truth to be told and all the facts to be put on the table. On the other hand, he is frightened that some of the facts (a particular lie, a certain sexual act) might be too painful for his wife to hear. *Should I hold back some of the truth? I've already hurt my wife so much. Is it fair to tell her information that won't change what happened but can only make her feel worse?*

5. A vicious cycle erupts. The unfaithful spouse, uncomfortable with providing explicit answers, gets a bit evasive. Or he simply does not remember the events in exact detail. The wife detects his evasiveness and is unwilling to accept "I don't remember" as an answer. So she presses for more information. She becomes finely attuned to any inconsistency in his story, much as an experienced interrogator would be. She asks the same questions over and over, implying that his previous answers weren't good enough. He is offended by that and starts to grow weary of the inquisition. He refuses to answer some questions on the grounds that she is becoming unreasonable in her approach. She views his unwillingness to cooperate as evidence that he has something more to hide, and persists in her questioning.

6. This vicious cycle proceeds in fits and starts. She tries to back down and stop asking so many questions, but eventually she can't help herself. He tries to be cooperative but gets angrier by the day that the affair isn't being put behind them. Occasionally he does remember a certain detail he previously had no memory of, intensifying her belief that he hides information to suit his needs.

    When rehashing past events accomplishes little, *the unfaithful spouse wants to focus on the future. The betrayed spouse is stuck in the past.* Eventually the unfaithful spouse develops an attitude of *I think I've paid for my crime.* He may not say those words, but he deep down feels he is being punished too harshly with no end in sight. She gets infuriated at his attitude and cannot fathom how weeks of interrogation could begin to pay for the anguish his infidelity has caused her. Consequently she resents him even more. *He has no understanding of what his affair has cost me,* she says to herself.

7. Eventually, if the couple is still together, she asks fewer questions and the couple tries to get on with their life together. But unexpectedly she may experience a flash-fire rage or deep depression. It might be that somehow she was reminded of the betrayal—an anniversary, a drive by the hotel her husband used, watching a movie where one of the characters has an affair—and for the time being it feels awful all over again. If the husband is with her at those moments, he gets angry that she can't let go of the past, that she won't forgive and forget, and *"Why did you have to ruin a perfectly good evening together by bringing up that topic!"* And she is angry that he doesn't understand.

Over a matter of months, the couple's interactions are often negative and tense. Moments of fun and leisure are rare. If the unfaithful spouse wants to do something enjoyable with his mate, she wonders how he could be so insensitive. *How can he expect me simply to have fun and enjoy his company right now?* If he does nothing, she wonders whether he cares, or she worries that their relationship is empty of fun and spontaneity.

Some of the more painful encounters occur when the betrayed spouse tries to "get to the bottom" of the affair by asking questions for which no answer is acceptable:

> *How could you risk destroying our lives and our children's lives by having an affair?*
> *Didn't your vows mean something to you?*
> *How could you lie to me when I asked you point-blank if you were having an affair?*
> *Why did you have an affair?*

Such questions are understandable, but any answer provided will be inadequate:

> *"If I had never found out about the affair, did you intend to keep it going forever?"*
> *"No, I mean I don't know. I never thought about how long it would last."*
> *"So it never occurred to you that the longer it went on the more damage you might do to this family?"*
> *"I said, 'I never thought about it,' damn it! What do you want me to say?"*
> *"I only want you to say the truth, but I guess that's too much to expect."*
> *"Here we go again. Look, I told you I'm sorry."*
> *"Sorry isn't good enough."*

Sorry *isn't* good enough. It is necessary but far from sufficient. The problem for betrayed spouses who want the marriage to survive is that their wish for a healed marriage collides with their wish to punish. And unfaithful spouses have an almost universal tendency to underestimate how much punishment they should receive for their crime, compared to the amount their partner feels is appropriate. See "Building a Successful Relationship" for suggestions on how best to handle the situation.

♥ ♥ ♥

BUILDING A SUCCESSFUL RELATIONSHIP

If one spouse has betrayed or repeatedly lied to his or her mate, and the partner feels compelled to interrogate and get to the "truth," the following guidelines should be followed.

1. The dishonest or unfaithful spouse should not complain that the punishment is worse than the crime. He or she should be willing to be receptive to any and all questions and answer them—even if they have been answered before. It is frustrating, but a small price to pay for a chance at healing the relationship.

2. The betrayed spouse is advised to schedule the question-answer periods. They can occur daily or weekly or monthly, but they should be scheduled. A time limit should be set (all-night marathons are not advisable). This provides the betrayed spouse with the necessary opportunity to ask questions and ventilate his or her feelings. It provides the other spouse the relief of knowing that the rest of the time can be spent free from rehashing the past.

   If the betrayed spouse thinks of something important to ask but the scheduled time to talk is not imminent, he should write it down and bring it up at the next scheduled discussion.

3. The betrayed spouse should have final say over how often they talk but is advised not to schedule meetings at particularly inopportune times—the middle of the night, during the partner's work day, etc.

If partners agree to the above guidelines and follow them, an improvement in the emotional climate is frequently noticeable within a few days.

♥ ♥ ♥

Will Trust Ever Return?

Trust can return, but it takes quite some time. A mistake couples make is to presume that trust must be "all or nothing." Realistically, a betrayed wife can learn to trust her husband more and more, but some events—a week-long business trip, his having lunch with a female coworker—may be too much to bear, at least for the time being. When rebuilding trust it is possible to arrive at an 85 percent trust level but the last fifteen percentage points may take years to achieve, depending upon the nature of the betrayal or dishonesty. (Analogously, anyone who has had difficulty losing weight will tell you that the last ten or fifteen pounds are the hardest to lose.)

The spouse who was unfaithful should earn back some trust by staying away from the affairee, just as a problem-drinker must stay away from bars, and a person who lied about gambling must stay away from the race track. That isn't always easy if the affairees work together. Often the person who had an affair (and now wishes to reconcile with his or her spouse) does not wish to act rudely or unkindly to the affairee. So, should they meet unexpectedly in the office corridor or in a department store, he or she will try to be polite and cordial. The betrayed spouse is uncomfortable with the thought of any chance meetings between the affairees, and sometimes unrealistically demands that steps be taken to avoid all chance encounters. The best rule to follow is for the unfaithful spouse to report any meetings or phone calls he or she may have had with the affairee. A spouse may be uncomfortable hearing of such encounters but will feel more trusting if the encounters are reported *voluntarily* (without her having to ask). If a betrayed husband or wife has to "pull teeth" to learn that his or her mate spoke on the phone with the affairee, trust will diminish and more arguments will erupt.

There is no good-enough reason why a spouse has an affair. The unfaithful spouse may point to reasons ("Our marriage was unsatisfying" or "It was a one-night stand, I was drunk, I didn't know what I was doing . . .") but the betrayed spouse will not accept any reason as sufficient. The unfaithful spouse must take full responsibility for the affair. No one "made me do it." Still, if there were marital difficulties, the betrayed spouse can feel more trusting if efforts are made to improve the problems that existed prior to the affair. While the unfaithful spouse assumes responsibility for the affair, both partners must accept responsibility for their role in the less-than-satisfying marriage. The problem, however, is that it's difficult to focus on issues like "poor communication" or "sexual incompatibility" when one is still stinging from the effects of the affair. Consequently, it may be a matter of months before couples can focus on the entire marriage, not just the infidelity.

Getting to the Heart of the Matter

When Julia first confronted Ryan about his affair, he denied it. "You must believe me," he said, and she did. But over time the evidence was too compelling: either he had been lying and unfaithful, or she was certifiably paranoid. Her best friend assured her she was not crazy, and she told Ryan that unless he told her the truth she would leave him. So he confessed.

What made it particularly painful was that it wasn't the first time this had happened to her. Before they married he had had a brief affair, which he admitted but attributed to a need for a "final fling" before marriage. She didn't like it, but she forgave him. And in the final year of her previous marriage, her former husband had also been unfaithful. At the time their marriage was probably headed for divorce anyway, but her ex's affair clinched it. It felt awful way back then, and it felt worse now.

By the time they came for therapy, Ryan had ended the affair. (It is difficult, if not impossible, truly, to work on a wounded marriage if the affair is continuing.) But Ryan still had feelings for Christine. Their main obstacles to trying to heal the marriage were Julia's total inability to trust Ryan and his total inability to forget about Christine. It had been four months since the affair was exposed and ended, but little good had been accomplished since then. Ryan and Julia both wanted their relationship to succeed, but each had little faith it could.

Applying the Formula

Step One: Unhooking Emotional Triangles

The goal of therapy was to help the two of them overcome the immediate obstacles to healing their relationship: Ryan needed to think more about Julia and less about Christine, and Julia needed to feel more trusting of Ryan. Whether the marriage would still survive once those goals were reached was anybody's guess.

There were two emotional triangles. The first was the obvious Ryan-Julia-Christine triangle. Since time spent with Julia was laden with conflict, Ryan's thoughts of Christine only increased. Occasionally Christine would call Ryan, ostensibly to find out how he was doing since their affair ended. Hearing her voice only made him compare her to Julia, and Julia always came in second.

The second triangle was Ryan-Julia-Julia's parents. Julia had confided in them recently. Like most parents, they felt concern for their daughter and supported her emotionally. They acted cold toward Ryan. While receiving support from her parents seemed helpful, Julia often came away from such encounters feeling worse about Ryan. She'd spend more time talking with her parents about Ryan than talking with Ryan about their marriage.

As painful as it was for Julia to realize that Ryan was a bit saddened at losing Christine, she understood that simply ordering him to forget about Christine would be useless—and likely counterproductive. It was agreed that Ryan would have some individual therapy sessions to discuss his feelings about his break up with Christine. Ryan also agreed that he would no longer accept phone calls from Christine. He wouldn't be rude, but he would be firm that his desire was now to focus on his relationship with his wife. He would hang up on Christine if necessary. He also agreed to inform Julia of any phone call he received from Christine and repeat to her what was said in the conversation. Julia agreed that she would not be quick to criticize Ryan for things he said (or didn't say) to Christine. Julia understood that her constant criticism, while understandable, was an obstacle to improving their relationship.

Julia also agreed to speak less frequently and less in-depth with her parents. Mostly she would tell them, "We're in therapy now, trying to improve matters" and let it go at that. When her parents criticized Ryan (which they often did since learning of his affair), Julia would tell them that while she understood their anger, it didn't help her to hear their criticisms.

By unhooking themselves from the two triangles, Julia and Ryan improved the odds that they could deal cleanly with their relationship, unhindered by others.

Step Two: Examining Your Role in the Problem

Ryan's tendency (before the affair) was to withdraw from conflict. That was a contributing factor to why their relationship was less than satisfactory. Ryan's withdrawal only heightened Julia's fear that he didn't care, which caused her to overreact to small inconsiderate acts, which caused Ryan to withdraw further. Since the exposure of the affair, his way of coping hadn't changed. Whenever Julia wanted to discuss the affair, he'd try to end the conversation early or tune her out completely. That only heightened Julia's fear that he was hiding something, causing her to confront him even more.

The more she confronted, the more he withdrew, and vice versa. So Ryan agreed to talk with Julia about the affair.

Julia understood that her spontaneous eruptions of anger and need to talk often diminished any positive interactions they might have. They might be having a pleasant dinner together when Julia would see a need to interrogate Ryan about one of his lies. So Julia agreed to schedule her discussions at preagreed times. That way she could be assured of having time to discuss the affair and he could be assured of time together spent doing other things.

As Ryan cooperated with Julia's need to ask him questions about the affair, she stopped feeling he was trying to hide things from her, and her trust of him began to increase.

Step Three: Uncovering Hidden Agendas

At this point, any disagreement or question was about deeper issues. If Ryan arrived home later than expected and Julia asked him what took him so long, she was really asking, *"How can I trust you?"* If he wanted to spend some time alone, she'd wonder *Does he really care about me anymore?*

Ryan was never sure just how much Julia loved him. And he also felt restricted, controlled by her as she'd inquire about his day in great detail.

They mutually agreed not to criticize one another for "making a big deal" out of minor events. They fully understood that no event was minor anymore. Until the inflammation from the wound of the affair lessened, each would overreact to certain events. Therapy helped them to understand that *the real problem was not overreacting to some event but criticizing their partner for overreacting.* By being understanding and less emotional about their partner's occasional overreactions, they each helped to lessen the inflammation.

Step Four: Examining Your Past

I asked Ryan to think about different times in his life when he was confronted with a difficulty—a problem in school, conflict with friends or family, etc. Then I asked him to recall how he coped with that difficulty. Did he *fight? flee? freeze? fold?* Ryan recalled how in college he received a "B" for a course in his major field. Believing that a "B" was equivalent to failing, he changed majors to a course of study he believed he could get all "As" in. In essence, Ryan chose to *flee* rather than study harder in his chosen field.

It was apparent to Ryan that as he became somewhat unhappy in his marriage, he looked for another relationship rather than work harder at the one he was already in. Initially, he'd told himself that maybe he and Julia weren't meant for one another. Now, he wondered if perhaps they might be compatible—if he would make the effort to work on improving the relationship instead of fleeing from it.

By following the four steps listed above, Julia and Ryan had their best chance to halt the recurrent conflict about his affair. But they still had work to do. Communication skills needed polishing, and they had grown apart the past few years—each less interested in the other. They each needed to feel more cared about by the other. Ryan recognized that it would be harder for Julia to show caring while the memory of his affair was still fresh in her mind, but he intended to show more caring for her. Each realized that it could take a year or so before the marriage was fully on the right track, and that the memory of the betrayal would live long after that.

Keep in Mind

- Trust is the keystone of a committed relationship. Without it, good communication skills, sexual compatibility, and a capacity to enjoy each other's company have little meaning.

- An unreliable spouse can cause as much damage to a relationship as an unfaithful spouse.

- You will have to act as if you trust your mate before you can feel trusting.

- Forgiveness isn't easy and can take time. It begins as a decision—a willingness to be forgiving—even though you don't *feel* forgiving just yet. It helps a lot if the one who hurt you is sincerely remorseful.

Chapter 16

How to Hang in There:
Four Additional Guidelines

Relationship problems persist not because of the nature of the difficulties, but because of the manner in which those difficulties get handled. People misidentify the essential problem of their relationship, apply solutions that won't work, and reapply those solutions when the desired effect doesn't occur. Then they blame their partner for being stubborn, malicious, or unwilling to cooperate. Feeling unfairly blamed and misunderstood, the other partner gets angry and cynical, only adding to the negative climate.

With the right approach, a downward spiral can reverse itself. Positive gestures will beget positive gestures. Solutions to thorny problems will easily fall into place. And even troublesome personality differences may fade.

"Once we improved our communication skills and ended repetitive arguments a curious thing happened," one man said. "I used to need to socialize every weekend. Now I like staying home more with my wife. And she used to criticize me for liking Rush Limbaugh. Now she's one of his fans."

Once people discover what they must do to bring about genuine and positive change, they often realize that the right answers were with them all along. Instinctively, many people understand that to get along in this world—with your spouse, your family, your neighbor, and all other humans—there are some basic things that must be done:

- Examine your role in a problem before reflexively blaming others.
- Admit it when you're wrong.
- Act with kindness and consideration whenever possible.
- Be a committed parent to your children.
- Make sacrifices for your children's sake. Teach them that there is something to live for besides oneself.
- Work hard at something that provides meaning to your life. Encourage that which is good, don't simply discourage that which is not good.
- Say what you mean and mean what you say. Be someone others regard as honest and reliable.
- Honor the spiritual needs of others.
- Thank God.

Initiating positive change isn't always easy but it isn't the hardest part, either. *Maintaining those changes* is the hardest part. Just look at how people stumble when they try to keep doing the things they *know* are healthy: not overeating, drinking less, exercising more, having regular dental and medical checkups. When it comes to putting your relationships back on track, it requires perseverance in the face of pressure to give up.

Why People Give up Too Quickly

"It doesn't feel . . . natural," Pete explained to me. "You want me to listen to Anna and then summarize what I hear her telling me *before* I explain my point of view?"

Pete was accurately describing the technique of *reflective listening,* which helps assure couples that they are truly being understood by their partner.

"Yes, Pete. I know it feels unnatural and contrived," I said. "But up until now you and Anna argued, interrupted one another, and came away from discussions feeling misunderstood and uncared for."

"You got that right," Anna interjected.

"By using the tool of reflective listening, you can reduce arguments and increase understanding. And you'll probably feel cared about, too."

But Pete had a point. Reflective listening is a technique that couples often feel self-conscious about applying. Let's face it, summarizing what you hear before you give your point of view is something that only therapists and a few talk-show hosts do. Most people don't talk that way.

"We should already know how to talk," Anna said. "We've talked all our lives. We each have friends and family we've been able to speak to and understand. Something must be wrong, that Pete and I can't talk without arguing. Maybe reflective listening really won't help. Our problem must go deeper."

"You've walked most of your life, too," I replied. "But if you were in a serious accident or suffered a stroke, you might require physical therapy to help you learn to walk all over again. I don't expect that you and Pete will always have to use reflective listening. But for the next couple of months I think it would be of great benefit. Thereafter, if you and Pete are at odds with one another, use reflective listening the way you might use a standby prescription of antibiotics in your medicine cabinet. Take it when you need it."

Pete and Anna had honed in on a common concern among people trying to change their way of relating. Use of any technique or strategy does feel contrived and will make them more self-conscious. For example, I often ask couples to increase their show of caring or affection for one another. So when a usually unromantic wife greets her husband with a wet kiss, both of them are self-conscious. *Is she doing this because she really wants to?* the husband wonders. *Or is she only doing it because the doctor told her to?*

I often find it necessary to remind a couple that to second-guess a partner's motive for following a therapeutic prescription misses the point. *"Give your partner credit for attempting the technique,"* I say. *"After all, no one is forcing him or her to do it."*

It is precisely because of this self-consciousness that some couples stop applying effective techniques. They then blame the technique as unnatural or ineffective, when the real problem is their own anxiety about using it.

So the first guideline to follow when trying to "hang in there" is this: *If you're self-conscious about applying a technique, do it anyway.* Allow yourselves to feel self-conscious instead of criticizing one another for it. It is okay and normal to think that applying a new strategy is somehow awkward or contrived. With time and practice, it will seem like second nature.

A second helpful guideline to "hang in there" is to *handle a relationship conflict the way you know is right, regardless of how well or poorly your mate is handling it.*

Too often partners give up trying because they perceive their mate as having given up. While the relationship will not survive if only one of you works on it, each of you will from time to time mishandle a situation. You'll say or do the wrong thing—and know you are doing so—but you won't stop yourself. You'll judge when you should be trying to understand. You'll interrupt when you should be listening. You'll accuse when you should be examining your role in the problem. You'll withdraw when you should be connecting.

The longer you and your mate have mishandled conflict, the more mixed your feelings will be about trying to improve matters. (It is no accident that precisely when an uncooperative spouse decides to cooperate, his or her mate says, "Sorry, I gave you your chance.") Each of you is ambivalent, but you arrange to make it look as if you are willing to work on the relationship but your partner is not. If you and your mate are frequently out of sync with one another—he's ready for a weekend trip to smooth things over, you're not; you're ready to talk, he's not—then each of you is holding back on the relationship but blaming it on the other.

The only way out of this trap is to not make your positive, constructive behavior contingent upon what your mate does. Try to do the right thing even if your mate is not fully cooperative.

If she's loud and angry, hear her out rather than accuse her of being uncaring. Look for the merit of what she's saying and comment on that first.

If he refuses to talk, inform him that you'll give him time to think but that, without a dialogue, there will be no opportunity for understanding.

Your partner may never tell you this, but often he is secretly happy and relieved to discover that you can cooperate with him, even when he is being uncooperative. Under such circumstances he will appraise you differently:

"After what I just said, I wouldn't blame her for leaving. But she didn't leave. Maybe she really does care."

♥ ♥ ♥

BUILDING A SUCCESSFUL RELATIONSHIP

If you find you can't "hang in there" when your mate is being particularly uncooperative, and if your mate feels the same way with regard to you, try this approach:

Split the week. You take Monday, Tuesday, and Wednesday. He takes Thursday, Friday, and Saturday. On your days you are required to be cooperative and use constructive communication and caring techniques *regardless of how uncooperative your partner is.* Such a strategy (yes, it is contrived and unnatural—so what?) helps insure that one of you will do the right things on any given day. Often, hanging in there like that helps a reluctant spouse to get back on the right track. By splitting the week, the burden of always being the "strong" one isn't on your shoulders. It becomes a shared responsibility that minimizes the likelihood of mutual withdrawal and uncooperativeness.

♥ ♥ ♥

A third effective tool to help you stay on track is to *boost your sense of optimism.* Research shows that pessimists are likely to give up when the going gets tough. Optimists tend to persevere. Both attitudes create a self-fulfilling prophecy: When efforts are abandoned too soon, matters don't work out, which leads to pessimism; whereas perseverance increases the odds matters can work out, thereby engendering optimism.

In my book *Life's Parachutes: How to Land on Your Feet During Trying Times,* I showed that hope and optimism have four underpinnings.

1. Hope takes root when you begin to feel *understood.* By using effective communication techniques and by trying to see the merit to your partner's point of view, you create understanding. Unhappy couples rarely feel understood by one another. Instead they feel discredited. To understand is not necessarily to agree with; it is simply to hear without judging.

2. Hope and optimism increase as your *faith* in your ability to handle conflict increases. By persevering, effective conflict-resolution skills can be finely tuned, increasing your faith in their effectiveness.

3. Optimism requires committed work. Despite setbacks, which are universal, you have to be willing to put forth the effort, even though you may be cynical. It is ironic that many couples seem to halt their efforts *at the crucial moment when a breakthrough is about to occur.* Not wanting to succeed and then be let down by another setback, some couples hold back when success is imminent—thereby insuring that they will not make progress.

4. Optimism is nourished when there is *meaning* to your hard work. To persevere you must not only *persist,* you must have a *purpose.* The divorce rate is lower for couples with children precisely because they are willing to try harder for their children's sake. Children often provide a couple with the purpose they need to persevere. Other people persevere because they know they possess some personal flaws that will accompany them to the next relationship. It seems more valuable to improve themselves now, in their current relationship, than to attempt to do so in the next relationship.

Optimists have an almost universal tendency to view problems as temporary. Pessimists view them as permanent. Challenging yourself to believe that all problems are temporary can enhance your optimism and improve your endurance.

The Fourth Guideline

So, to persevere in your effort to make positive changes in your relationship, it is important to:

1. Refuse to allow the fact that some techniques feel contrived or unnatural to dissuade you from using them.
2. Use the techniques even if your mate is uncooperative.
3. Remind yourself that all problems are temporary and that tools do exist to help you in your relationship.

Lastly, it is important (even if a tad inconvenient) to have regular progress checks. Research shows that without a follow-up evaluation, 50 percent of couples who've successfully made changes in their relationship will relapse. Touching base with one another on a regular (at *least* weekly) basis will help alert you to small problems before they become big ones. Once progress has been maintained for about three months, it is all right to reduce the frequency of the checkups.

A checkup need not be a big deal. If all seems to be going well, simply saying to your mate, "I like the way things went this week. Did you?" may be all that is required. If there were problems or concerns, the discussion need not be overly serious. Do something enjoyable together while discussing matters. Go for a stroll. Rub each other's back. Go out for ice cream. Sitting across from the dining room table with a note-pad may be efficient, but it will be ineffective if the tone of the meeting is too serious or formal.

During a feedback session, predict upcoming events that might throw you off track. Are in-laws visiting? Will that pose a problem? If so, how do the two of you plan to deal with it? Any change in the children's school schedule? Changes in your work schedule? Planning on going on a diet? Quitting smoking? Any of these can be potential stressors that could upset the marital apple cart. Planning ahead can prevent unnecessary complications.

When All Is Said and Done . . .

. . . Your repetitive arguments really can stop. For good. And your relationship really can blossom. By learning how to get to the heart of the matter, you can halt the merry-go-round of unproductive arguments and standoffs. Once that happens, you will view your mate from a different perspective—with more understanding and less judgment, with less resentment and more love.

Start today. Speak from your heart, and make all you do matter.

Keep in Mind

- Hang in there. Your reaction to a setback is more important than the setback itself.
- Follow the "Thirty-Day Rule." Apply a technique for at least thirty days before you abandon it. Some techniques take time to learn and time to have an impact.
- When a setback occurs, don't lose sight of the positive changes that have also occurred. If the overall trend has been positive, you have reason to be optimistic.

Notes

Chapter 3. The Conflict Styles of Dissatisfied Couples

[1] Hetherington, Cox, and Cox, "Effects of Divorce on Parents and Children."

[2] Christenson, "Dysfunctional Interaction Patterns in Couples."

[3] Stafford and Canary, "Maintenance Strategies and Romantic Relationship Type, Gender and Relational Characteristics."

Chapter 4. Common Patterns of Endless Arguments

[1] Gottman and Levenson, "Assessing the Role of Emotion in Marriage."

[2] Roberts and Krokoff, "A Time-Series Analysis of Withdrawal, Hostility, and Displeasure in Satisfying and Dissatisfying Marriages."

Chapter 6. The Second Step: Changing Your Role in the Problem

[1] Jacobsen, Follette, and MacDonald, "Reactivity to Positive and Negative Behavior in Distressed and Nondistressed Married Couples."

Chapter 7. The Third Step: Uncovering Hidden Agendas

[1] Kirchler, "Everyday Life Experiences at Home: An Interaction Diary Approach to Assessing Marital Relationships."

[2] Driscoll, *The Binds that Tie.*

Chapter 10. When Parenting Is the Problem

[1] Graham, "The Effects of Parent-Adolescent Communication on Adolescent Sexual Behavior."

[2] Vishner, *Old Loyalties, New Ties.*

Chapter 11. When Money Is the Problem

[1] This solution was proposed by Michael Whiner-Davis in his book *Divorce Busting.*

2Guerin, Fay, Burden, and Kautto, *The Evaluation and Treatment of Marital Conflict,* p. 57.

Chapter 14. When Balancing Career and Family Is the Problem

[1] Ross, Mirowski, and Huber, "Dividing Work, Sharing Work, and Inbetween: Marriage Patterns and Depression."

[2] Kessler and McRae, "The Effects of Wives' Employment on the Mental Health of Married Men and Women."

Bibliography

Atwood, Joan. "Effect of Premenstrual Mood Changes on the Couple Relationship." *The Family Psychologist* 7, no. 3 (1991): 17–19.

Bader, E., and P. Pearson. *In Quest of the Mythical Mate.* New York: Brunner/Mazel, 1988.

Beach, S.R., E. Sandeen, and K.D. O'Leary. *Depression In Marriage.* New York: Guilford, 1990.

Betcher, William, and Robie Macauley. *The Seven Basic Quarrels of Marriage.* New York: Ballantine Books, 1990.

Biernat, Monica, and Camille Wortman. "Sharing of Home Responsibilities between Professionally Employed Wives and Their Husbands." *Journal of Personality and Social Psychology* 60 (1991): 844–860.

Blumstein, Philip, and Pepper Schwartz. *American Couples.* New York: William Morrow, 1983.

Brothers, Barbara Jo. "Healthy Coupling . . . What Makes It?" *Journal of Couples Therapy* 1, no. 1 (1990): 11.

Bruno, Frank. *Psychological Symptoms.* New York: John Wiley and Sons, 1993.

Christner, Anne Marshall. Article appearing in *The Brown University Family Therapy Letter.* Providence, RI: Mannisses Communications Group, Inc., 1990.

Christenson, A. "Dysfunctional Interaction Patterns in Couples." In *Perspectives On Marital Interaction.* Edited by Noller and Fitzpatrick. Philadelphia: Multilingual Matters, Ltd., 1988.

Coleman, Paul. *The 30 Secrets of Happily Married Couples.* Holbrook, MA: Bob Adams, Inc., 1992.

Coleman, Paul. *Life's Parachutes: How To Land On Your Feet During Trying Times.* New York: Dell, 1993.

Driscoll, Richard. *The Binds that Tie.* Lexington, MA: Lexington Books, 1991.

Feinhauer, Leslie, Dale Lund, and Jean Miller. "Family Issues in Multigenerational Households." *American Journal of Family Therapy* 15, no. 1 (1987): 52–61.

Filson, E.E., and S.J. Thomas. "Behavioral Antecedents of Relationship Stability and Adjustment: A Five-Year Longitudinal Study." *Journal of Marriage and the Family* 50 (1988): 785–795.

Fincham, F., and T. Bradbury. *The Psychology of Marriage.* New York: Guilford, 1991.

Frank, E., C. Anderson, and D. Rubenstein. "Frequency of Sexual Dysfunction in 'Normal' Couples." *New England Journal of Medicine* 299 (1978): 111–115.

Gilbert, Roberta M. *Extraordinary Relationships.* Minneapolis: Chronimed Publishing, 1992.

Gottman, John. "How Marriage Changes." In *Depression and Aggression in Family Interactions.* Edited by Gerald R. Patterson. Hillsdale, NJ: Laurence Erlbaum Associates, 1990.

Gottman, J.M., and R.W. Levenson. "Assessing the Role of Emotion in Marriage." *Behavioral Assessment* 8 (1986): 31–48.

Graham, Melody. "The Effects of Parent-Adolescent Communication on Adolescent Sexual Behavior." Paper presented at the annual convention of the American Psychological Association, Washington, DC, 1992.

Greeley, Andrew. *Faithful Attraction: Discovering Intimacy, Love, and Fidelity in American Marriages.* New York: Tor, 1991.

Guerin, Philip, Leo Fay, Susan Burden, and Judith Kautto. *The Evaluation and Treatment of Marital Conflict.* New York: Basic Books, 1987.

Heitler, Susan. *From Conflict To Resolution.* New York: W.W. Norton, 1990.

Hetherington, E.M., M. Cox, and R. Cox. "Effects of Divorce on Parents and Children." In *Nontraditional Families.* Edited by M. Lamb. Hillsdale, NJ: Erlbaum Associates, 1981.

Jacobsen, N.S., V. Follette, and D. McDonald. "Reactivity to Positive and Negative Behavior in Distressed and Nondistressed Married Couples." *Journal of Consulting and Clinical Psychology* 50 (1982): 706–714.

Johnson, Catherine. *Lucky In Love.* New York: Viking Penguin, 1992.

Justice, Blair. *Who Gets Sick.* Los Angeles: Jeremy Tarcher, 1987.

Kerr, Michael, and Murray Bowen. *Family Evaluation.* New York: Norton, 1988.

Kessler, Ron, and James McRae. "The Effect of Wives' Employment on the Mental Health of Married Men and Women." *American Sociological Review* 47 (1982): 216–227.

Kiecolt-Glaser, J., R. Glaser, E. Shuttleworth, C. Dyer, P. Ogrocki, and C. Speicher. "Chronic Stress and Immunity in Caregivers of Alzheimer's Disease Victims." *Psychosomatic Medicine* 49 (1987): 523–535.

Kirchler, Erich. "Everyday Life Experiences at Home: An Interaction Diary Approach to Assessing Marital Relationships." *Journal of Family Psychology* 2, no. 3 (1989): 311–336.

Lauer, J. and R. Lauer. "Marriages Made to Last." *Psychology Today* (June 1985): 26.

McKinney, M.E., and H. White. "Dietary Habits and Blood Chemistry Levels of Stress Prone Individuals: The Hot Reactor." *Comprehensive Therapy* 11, no. 8 (1985): 21–28.

Napier, Augustus Y. *The Fragile Bond.* New York: Harper & Row, 1988.

Noller, Patricia, and Mary Anne Fitzpatrick. "Marital Communication in the Eighties." *Journal of Marriage and the Family* 52 (1990): 832–843.

Norval, Glenn D. "The Recent Trend in Marital Success in the U.S." *Journal of Marriage and the Family* 53 (1987): 261–270.

Norval, G., and K.B. Kramer. "The Marriages and Divorces of Children of Divorce." *Journal of Marriage and Family Therapy* 49 (1987): 811–825.

Norval, G., and S. McLanahan. "Children and Marital Happiness: A Further Specification of Relationships." *Journal of Marriage and the Family* 44 (1982): 63–72.

Norval, Glenn and Charles Weaver. "The Contribution of Marital Happiness to Global Happiness." *Journal of Marriage and the Family* 43, no. 1 (1981): 161–168.

Nowinski, Joseph. *A Lifelong Love Affair.* New York: Norton, 1988.

Rankin, R., and J. Maneker. "The Duration of Marriage in a Divorcing Population: The Impact of Children." *Journal of Marriage and the Family* 47 (1985): 43–52.

Roberts, Linda, and Lowell Krokoff. "A Time-Series Analysis of Withdrawal, Hostility, and Displeasure in Satisfying and Dissatisfying Marriages." *Journal of Marriage and the Family* 52 (1990): 95–105.

Ross, Catherine E., John Mirowsky, and Joan Huber. "Dividing Work, Sharing Work, and In-between: Marriage Patterns and Depression." *American Sociological Review* 48 (1983): 809–823.

Schacter, J., and K. O'Leary. "Affective Intent and Impact in Marital Communication." *American Journal of Family Therapy* 13, no. 4 (1985): 17–23.

Skeff, M., and L. Pearlin. "Caregiving: Role Engulfment and the Loss of Self." *The Gerontologist* 32 (1992): 656–664.

Snell, W.E. "The Masculine Role As a Moderator of Stress-Distress Relationships." Study cited in Blair Justice's *Who Gets Sick.* Los Angeles: Jeremy Tarcher, 1987.

Stafford, Laura, and Daniel Canary. "Maintenance Strategies and Romantic Relationship Type, Gender, and Relational Characteristics." *Journal of Social and Personal Relationships* 8 (1991): 217–242.

Sternberg, Daniel P., and Ernst G. Beier. "Changing Patterns of Conflict." *Journal of Communication* 27 (1977): 97–100.

Taffel, Ron. *Parenting By Heart.* Reading, MA: Addison-Wesley Publishing Co., 1991.

Toman, Walter. *Family Constellation.* New York: Springer Publishing, 1976.

Vishner, Emily and John Vishner. *Old Loyalties, New Ties.* New York: Brunner/Mazel, 1988.

Weiss, Robert. *Staying the Course: The Emotional and Social Lives of Men Who Do Well at Work.* New York: Free Press, 1990.

Whiner-Davis, Michael. *Divorce Busting.* New York: Summit Books, 1992.

White, L., A. Booth, and J. Edwards. "Children and Marital Happiness: Why the Negative Correlation?" *Journal of Family Issues* 7 (1986): 131–147.

White, Lynn, and Bruce Keith. "The Effects of Shift-Work on the Quality and Stability of Marital Relationships." *Journal of Marriage and the Family* 52 (1990): 457–462.

Yablonsky, Lewis. *The Emotional Meaning Of Money.* New York: Gardner Press, 1991.

Youngstrom, Nina. "Juggling Job and Family: Sensitive Employers Help." *APA Monitor* (December 1992): 33.

Zal, H. Michael. *The Sandwich Generation.* New York: Insight Books, 1992.

Zick, C.B., and J.L. McCullough. "Trends in Married Couples' Time Use: Evidence from 1977–1978 and 1987–1988." *Sex Roles 24 (1991): 459–48.*

Index